MURDER IN THE MONASTERY

There have been three enduring passions in Barun's life—advertising, acting and writing, and not necessarily in that order. With a Master's degree in English from Jadavpur University, Kolkata, he embarked upon a career in advertising that spanned more than three decades, winning him numerous accolades and awards as a Creative Director.

Acting happened in his career as a happy accident. Chosen by Satyajit Ray to play the protagonist in the film *Seemabaddha*, Barun came up with an inspiring performance as a high-flying executive that won him a special President's Award for acting. After a hiatus of nearly two decades, he returned to acting and has since tackled challenging roles in both Bollywood and Tollywood with equal aplomb, distinguishing himself in films as *Lootera*, *Roy*, *Chotushkone*, *Mishor Rohoshya*, *Bela Sheshe* and *Chorabali*.

The third passion in Barun's life has been writing. At one time a regular film reviewer, and contributor of feature articles in major dailies, he has so far published four highly acclaimed novels in Bengali. His work has played a major role in establishing the adult thriller genre in Bengali literature. *Murder in the Monastery* is his second book in English, the first being *Coke*.

MURDER IN THE MONASTERY

BARUN CHANDA

RUPA

Published by
Rupa Publications India Pvt. Ltd 2019
7/16, Ansari Road, Daryaganj
New Delhi 110002

Sales centres:
Allahabad Bengaluru Chennai
Hyderabad Jaipur Kathmandu
Kolkata Mumbai

ISBN: 978-93-5333-337-9

First impression 2019

10 9 8 7 6 5 4 3 2 1

The moral right of the author has been asserted.

Printed at HT Media Ltd. Gr. Noida

This book is dedicated to the sternest critic of my writings, my wife Manjusree, with the fond hope that one of these days she would soften up just a little bit.

That evening Avinash Roy locked the door of his guest room and prepared to go to the dining hall with somewhat mixed feelings. He had been here, at Dengziang Monastery, for more than a fortnight. Part of him, rejuvenated and revitalized by the cool, crisp mountain air and the enforced regular life of the hills, was raring to go back to work. Pure oxygen can have a high octane effect on your system. The other, having spent hours at Buddhist monasteries, had made him strangely reluctant to go back to civilization, to Kolkata. For going back would require him to deal on a daily basis with knaves, deviants, crooks, rapists and murderers, political criminals and corporate giants, who coolly defraud crores of public money without batting an eyelid.

The mere thought of going back to that life gave him the jitters. Ah well! *C'est la vie*. He gave the lock a smart tug to make sure it was properly secured and started whistling a tune.

Sharmila, his wife, walking a few steps behind him, arched her eyebrows in surprise. Why on earth her husband should want to whistle 'Raindrops keep falling on my head' on a frosty night like this was beyond her.

But then, in all the thirty-five years that she'd been with him, she had never been able to completely fathom him. Part of the charm, I suppose, she smiled to herself.

'Will you stop jangling the keys? I find it so irritating.'

He stopped fiddling with the keys with a look of injured innocence.

'But don't you think it makes for some very interesting percussion effects? Like playing castanets in flamenco?' He drummed his fingers over the keys once more for good effect.

'Well, not really.'

He fell silent. There was an air of finality in her voice that brooked no further arguments.

He swung the door open for her to enter the dining hall. Taking a couple of steps towards their usual table, he stopped in his tracks. It was already occupied.

Roy wasn't a fussy fellow at all. He would be the last person to create a scene over a trifling matter such as the holding up of a table. If anything, he abhorred making scenes. But over the last fortnight, guests had come to choose their own preferred tables in the dining hall. An unwritten code had been established. Perhaps one preferred a table by the window simply because it offered a better view of the mountains. Someone else might prefer one of the inner tables, because of its proximity to the fireplace.

Now, that unwritten code had been broken. A frown appeared on his brow as he noticed their table had been occupied by none other than the sour-faced, grumpy-looking couple who had checked in only a day ago. He recovered his composure soon and spotted an empty table further down the hall.

'Come, Sharmi, we'll go and sit there.'

Weaving his way past the tables, he greeted the lady at Table Number Two with a smile.

'Hello Miriam!'

This did not go down too well with Sharmi. In spite of the severe cut of her dress, Miriam was a rather attractive woman.

Table Number One was, as usual, unoccupied. No one wished to face a blast of ice-cold wind each time the dining room door swung open.

'Hello,' Miriam murmured shyly, averting her eyes.

Miriam de Gonzales was a Coorgi girl with a fair complexion and grey-green eyes. In fact, Avinash and Sharmi had privately wondered if she had some Spanish or Portuguese genes after all.

Miriam was probably in her late twenties, or early thirties; it was hard to tell. Though she wasn't a nun, there was something about her that reminded you of a Christian missionary. Perhaps it was her attire, the sack-like cut of her dress that did its best to hide the generous contours of her body from the public eye.

Table Number Three, was as usual, occupied by a rather dapper looking, middle-aged Frenchman.

'How's your film project coming up, Monsieur Duval?'

'Very well…very well, Mr Roy.'

While this was addressed to Roy, Duval's roving eyes were focused on Sharmila. Like all Frenchmen, he liked admiring good-looking women.

Pierre had introduced himself to everyone in Dengziang Monastery as a celebrated documentary filmmaker, working for National Geographic and Discovery Channel. Roy couldn't vouch for the veracity of the Frenchman's claims as he wasn't much of a television viewer. Truth be told, he didn't have the time for it.

His relationship with Pierre had remained formal and somewhat frosty, in spite of the latter's best efforts. The Frenchman had invited them to his room one evening to share a glass of wine and had been deeply disappointed when Sharmi didn't show up. He was even more disappointed to hear that she didn't drink at all.

'*Mon dieu! Elle ne boit pas!* How's that possible?'

He had spent the rest of the evening talking desultorily about the film project in hand. It was clear that the spirit had lost its fizz.

Roy gathered that he was here to shoot a documentary on the life of the Buddhist monks, with special emphasis on their formative years. He even had a title ready for this project—*The Little Buddhas of Dengziang*, which, come to think of it, wasn't a bad title at all.

But something had warned him, call it sixth sense, not to trust the Frenchman. Was it Pierre's unashamed admiration of Sharmila that had put him on his guard? Or, was it something else? He wasn't sure. For all his big talk, there was nothing much happening on the ground. For example, there was no movie camera, no director of photography, no crew, no recorder, no recordist. Nothing.

True, Pierre had claimed he was on a 'recce' tour this time. But strangely, he carried no pads, or dictaphones, took no notes and made no scribbles. He didn't even carry a still camera with him. And he seemed to spend too much time with the little lamas in their dorms. A trifle too much for Roy's liking.

At Table Number Four sat the big American, William 'Billy' Ford. Billy had a standard introduction for himself. 'I don't run an automotive empire. Nor am I into politics. Or, filmmaking for that matter. I am the little unsung Ford from the United States of America whom you're sure to hear more about in the future.'

Billy was a towering guy, 6'5" or 6'6" tall, with a frame to match. He had matted blonde hair, blonde eyebrows and blonde eyelashes. Even the furry hair on his forearms was blonde. He had a flying blue eagle tattooed on his right forearm. So, when he flapped his arms about, which he did all the time, the eagle would perform all kinds of impossible aerial feats, taking sudden dips, perilous turns, free falls and vertical take-offs, as if laws of gravitation didn't exist.

He had a pronounced American nasal drawl, which Roy didn't find particularly endearing. In any case, Roy had never been fond of American English. The way they pronounced the word 'schedule' would raise his hackles every time. What he found even less endearing was Billy's jokes. If he meant to convey the impression of an amiable American, he would actually be doing a pretty convincing job of being the very opposite.

He was an art collector. Or so he said. He claimed to be here in search of rare Tibetan tankhas and bronze figurines of Tara. Roy urged Sharmila to slip past Table Number Four with as much alacrity as decency would permit. But to no avail.

'Hi buddy!' Billy roared, extending a massive arm to block their passage. 'Why don't the two of you sit down at my table? We got a lotta catching up to do.'

'Sorry Billy,' quipped Roy, 'not enough space at your table.'

This, in point of fact, was not untrue. Billy's huge frame had gobbled up the entire of Table Number Four.

'Haw haw haw!' He roared again, but this time in mirth. 'That's a good one. Haw haw.'

Even without looking, Roy could feel all eyes in the dining room boring down on them, and he positively abhorred it.

He walked past Table Number Five without wishing the European couple. His earlier efforts in making friends with them had failed miserably. When he had wished them 'good morning' during breakfast that day, they hadn't even bothered to acknowledge it. As if they had heard nothing.

Roy had unashamedly eavesdropped on them when they were talking at the reception desk. The man had spoken haltingly, in broken English. The woman hadn't spoken at all. Not even to her husband. Maybe she was born mute. And when the husband had mumbled something to her, it was neither in French, nor German, Spanish or Italian. Maybe they were from Eastern Europe, Poland or Romania. Maybe if he could somehow get a look at the register book, he would know.

Sharmi didn't approve of her husband's habit of snooping around. But he couldn't help it. The very nature of his work habituated him to observe people he met in daily life, and if necessary, spy on them.

When the two of them finally sat down, he gloomily reflected that their table was farthest from the lone fireplace in the dining room. The sight of the crackling fireplace, and their distance from it, stoked his misery further. As they waited for the food to arrive, all he could do was make a funnel out of the palm of his hands and blow hard into them. As for her, she wrapped the pashmina shawl tightly around herself and shivered demurely.

The soup, when it arrived, was only lukewarm. Maybe it had been lying in the pantry for a while. Or maybe the cook had forgotten to reheat the soup before serving. The rest of the meal didn't add up to much either—some vegetables, mostly cabbage which he detested, a few peas and stale-looking carrots. The main course consisted of chicken roast—stringy and anything but tender—and two pieces of bread and butter. The meal was rounded off with caramel custard as dessert, which was just about so-so.

But he wasn't complaining. The last fifteen days had been the most refreshing that he could remember in a long time.

Before undertaking the trip to Sikkim, he had visited Motilal Benarasidas, a bookshop in Camac Street which specialized in Indology. Here he had come across a fascinating collection of Buddhist literature that could easily last him the next six months. In the end, he had restricted himself to buying just three books—one on the life of Buddha, the second on the Dalai Lama and the third one called *The Dialogues of the Buddha*.

Sharmi's heart sank when she noticed the books being packed in his suitcase. She had hoped so much to have him to herself on this trip. Her fears were further compounded when she found that they were going to stay at a guest house within the Dengziang Monastery itself. Was her husband about to embrace Buddhism? Her alarms were, however, soon to be dispelled. To her pleasant surprise, she realized that reading up on Buddhist literature hadn't, in any way, affected her husband's sexual ardour.

At the monastery they were received by a young lama, named Chorten, who showed them to their rooms and made them comfortable with a welcome drink of Temi tea. Everywhere in the hills, Roy noticed, it was common practice to welcome guests with traditional tea. Later that day the young lama took them to a 'conducted' tour of the monastery. Dengziang had apparently been built more than three hundred years ago. Though smaller than Rhumtek, it was more beautiful. The monastery, he pointed out, had a three-tiered structure. The ground floor housed the main prayer hall and the figures of Guru Rimpoche and his consorts. The walls on this floor depicted impressive frescoes of Buddha and innumerable forms of the Bodhisatta.

'Take a closer look, sir,' Chorten had pointed at the walls, 'there are hundreds of faces of Buddha and hundreds of mandalas. No two are identical.' Sharmi and Roy spent the next ten minutes scrutinizing the walls, and had to admit he was right. Up on the first floor were the scriptures and an array of beautiful bronze statues, which had taken a bluish tinge with age. The third tier was the most impressive of all, containing an intricate wooden structure, representing the seven stages of heaven. Roy smiled to himself as he listened to Chorten. He knew that Dengziang followed the Tibetan form of Buddhism, which had a lot of tantric elements in it. Tara as Guru Rimpoche's consort was nothing but Goddess Kali corresponding to the Hindu religion. But, he had no wish to get drawn into a theological discourse on this subject.

Next morning Avinash woke up at the crack of dawn, when the spectacle of the majestic, snow-tipped Kanchenjunga was in full view. Clad in zipped-up thermal-lined 'cheaters', loose tweed trousers and cork-sole boots—most of them bought for him by his son at the spring sales in Illinois—Roy would go out for long walks down the meandering road. Here, mist clung to the trees till late in the morning, making them look like giant candyfloss. By the time Roy returned from his walks he would be ravenously hungry.

After breakfast, Sharmi would repair to their bedroom and stand by the window. Kanchenjunga was still in view. No longer pink-hued now, but still majestic.

Suddenly, without warning, Avinash would come and take her from behind.

'What are you doing?' She'd say exasperated. 'This is preposterous! Stop it...let go of me!'

As she tried to squirm out of his grip, he would pull her firmly back to him. And soon enough, her protestations would be drowned in cries and whispers of pleasure. There was also that other time, the very thought of which made her feel hot and clammy inside even now.

One day, after breakfast, they had decided to go out for a long stroll. No fixed destination. No sightseeing. Just a walk for pleasure. Their leisurely stroll had taken them to the middle of a forest, with not a soul around. There was a mountain stream flowing by. They had decided to take their shoes and socks off and sink their feet into the water. Their first contact with it was like an electric shock. The water was freezing cold! But once they got used to it, it was quite refreshing. They sat there for a long time, doing nothing. Sometime later, Roy looked at his watch and said it was time for them to return. On their way back, Roy suddenly stopped and turned to her.

'Supposing I make love to you now, right here?'

'Don't be ridiculous.' She kept on walking.

'No, I mean it.'

She turned around to him and said, 'Come on, Avinash, I am

hungry. Let's go back to the guest house.'

She wasn't at all prepared for what happened next. Roy pinned her to a tree trunk with his body.

'You're not serious.' She looked straight into his eyes.

He looked back with a deadpan face. 'I've never been more serious.'

There, in the middle of the forest, with a thousand birds as witness, he started to kiss her, first on her lips. Then he deftly pushed back her hair to kiss her on the nape of her neck. She shivered uncontrollably. It was one of her most erogenous zones. And he knew it. He lowered himself to unbutton her cardigan and started kissing her belly button. Her whole body quivered.

'Don't, please…' She said in a muffled voice. But, by then, his face had slid further down and she had to literally grab him by the hair, for, otherwise, she would surely have collapsed on the ground.

Other than rediscovering his long-lost libido, by a happy accident, Roy had chanced upon something else here as well, something that very few people find in a lifetime. Solitude. He felt at peace with himself.

If you asked him he wouldn't be able to explain how it had happened. He wasn't an overtly religious person. During the Durga puja, when Sharmi bathed early in the morning, changed into new clothes and fasted till the pushpanjali was over, he would simply laze about on the bed, consuming cup after cup of Orange Pekoe.

But, here, in a remote hill station in Sikkim, he had come upon a small nameless Buddhist monastery that gave him a wonderful, if somewhat frightening, experience. As one came out of Dengziang Monastery and walked towards the township, one came across a pathway on the left that snaked down to a small cluster of hutments. One morning, after breakfast, Roy followed this trail just out of curiosity. As he made his way through the dense foliage, mindful of the irregular steps, he came upon a stretch of level ground. To the left was a two-storied concrete building, standing at odds with the nearby tiled-roof hutments. To its right stood a quaint little monastery. Intrigued, he walked around it and came back to stand at the entrance. The door was padlocked.

Was it a private monastery, then? He looked around. There was this one concrete house nearby. He walked across to the house and knocked on the door. Presently, an elderly gentleman in traditional Sikkimese attire opened it.

'Yes?' The man looked enquiringly at him.

For a brief moment he was at a loss for words.

'Oh! I'm...I'm just a tourist from Calcutta. And I came upon this beautiful monastery. 'I was just wondering if it belonged to you.'

'Come,' the elderly gentleman ushered him in. 'The monastery indeed is ours, built by my father. You want to take a look? But first let me fix some tea for you.'

It seemed that the gentleman was seeking company. As they sipped tea and munched on biscuits, the gentleman talked about himself. Suraj Kiran Rumba, the gentleman, lived virtually alone here. He had two children—one worked in Mumbai and the other one was a school teacher in Darjeeling.

'And your wife?' Avinash gently enquired.

'Oh! She's in Gangtok...works for the Education Ministry. Actually, she's an IAS officer,' Suraj smiled diffidently.

After tea, he opened the monastery for Avinash and accompanied him to the prayer hall upstairs.

'Stay here as long as you wish.'

So saying, the gentleman retreated downstairs, leaving Roy alone in the prayer hall. The stairs were very steep and he had to take a minute to catch his breath. Through the sound of his pounding heartbeat, he could hear the sound of the gentleman's retreating footsteps.

Soon the monastery was enveloped in silence. Not knowing what to do, Avinash sat down on the wooden floor, allowing his back to rest against the wall. The pounding of his heart had somewhat subsided by then. He sat down cross-legged. Avinash wasn't in the habit of practising yoga, so he was pleasantly surprised with himself.

But here, without knowing why or how, Avinash had sat down on the wooden floor, allowing the sole of his feet to face upwards. How it happened he couldn't quite explain. But, in that moment, it just seemed the natural thing to do.

A shaft of blue light fell miraculously `on the floor through a small opening near the ceiling. The light looked diaphanous, like an illusion. His eyes closed gently, of their own accord. Avinash sat there, apparently in a trance, god knows for how long. When he came back to his senses it was noon. The feeling that he had was one of infinite lightness, as though he was levitating. At the same time it was scary. He had never experienced anything like this before.

Avinash came down the staircase, still in a bit of a daze. The elderly gentleman was waiting for him outside.

'Come here as often as you wish.' He smiled gently. 'People don't come here much. They prefer to visit Dengziang.'

Was it the elderly man's loneliness that made him seek Avinash's company? Or, had he seen something special in the latter which he recognized—a search for peace within himself?

On his way back to the guest house, Avinash figured he might have enough time to squeeze in just one more visit to this private monastery in the morning. This was their last night at Dengziang Monastery. Next day they were to have an early lunch before taking a cab to New Jalpaiguri. There, they were to board the Darjeeling Mail in the evening that would take them to Kolkata early next morning.

On returning to their room after dinner, Sharmi decided to finish the packing that night itself.

'What's the hurry, darling?' Avinash was feeling lazy after dinner. 'We could do the packing tomorrow morning as well.'

But Sharmi had decided otherwise. Stubbornly she said, 'If you don't feel up to it, I'll do the packing all by myself.'

This suited Avinash very well. Propping up a couple of pillows in one corner of the bed, he sat idly, a book in hand, while Sharmi took all the clothes out of the wardrobe and spread them on the bed. Avinash watched, fascinated as Sharmi folded each garment neatly into stacks before arranging them inside the suitcase. There was a certain sinewy suppleness about her that Avinash found disconcertingly attractive. Slowly he could feel desire welling up inside him.

Maybe it was sheer instinct, but Sharmila happened to look up at him just that very moment.

'What! Why are you staring at me like that?'

In a fraction of a second her face had flushed deeply, to the roots of her hair. She knew that look in her husband's eyes very well.

Avinash felt a mad desire to pick her up, lay her down on the bed and make love to her among the heap of scattered clothes.

Just then there was a gentle knock on the door. Both of them froze mid-air, as if caught in a guilty act.

'Who could it be at this time of the night?' Avinash whispered to Sharmi.

'How should I know?' Sharmi whispered back.

Both of them looked askance at each other and then towards

the door. Somebody coughed outside. Then there was another knock on the door.

'Mr Roy?' the voice enquired.

Reluctantly, Avinash got up and opened the door. Standing outside the door was a young lama. His face looked familiar. Avinash had met him there a couple of times and exchanged smiles. He didn't know the monk's name, or what he did there.

'Yes?' Avinash looked testily at the lama.

'Sir,' the monk bowed deeply and carried on, 'the chief of our Dengziang Monastery, Lama Phunsok, would like to speak with you. If you could spare a little time…'

If Lama Phunsok wanted to talk to Roy why hadn't he sent Lama Chorten? The first day they had come over to Dengziang, Lama Phunsok had engaged the former to take them around the monastery. Since then, a rapport had developed between them.

Avinash looked undecidedly at Sharmila and shrugged.

'He also sends profuse apologies for this rude intrusion.'

Lama Phunsok was engrossed in a book when Roy and the young lama entered the room.

'Sir,' the young lama's voice was soft and hesitant, 'Mr Roy is here.'

The venerable lama raised his head and looked at Avinash. Years of exposure to the sun at high altitude had given him a deep copper tan. In comparison, his arms, protected by the golden yellow and maroon robe, looked fair and almost feminine. His broad, flat face bespoke of Lepcha origin. Behind the glasses, his eyes looked large and compassionate, but also troubled. Seeing Roy, Lama Phunsok's leathery face broke into a smile.

'Thank you so much for coming. I wasn't sure you would.'

Lama Phunsok got up stiffly from the chair and extended his arms in a gesture of warm welcome.

'It's the gout. Some winters it gets bad. But otherwise…'

There ensued an awkward silence. Smiling, he turned towards the young monk.

'That would be all, Tenzing. You are free to leave now.'

The young monk bowed deeply, and silently left the room, closing the door gently behind him. For a while Lama Phunsok stared at it, deliberating whether to lock it from inside or not. Finally, he went slowly to the door and bolted it.

The room had a spacious cheerfulness about it. Silk tankhas draped the wall. A large crimson carpet lay spread out on the floor. A mustard-coloured dragon spat orange flames from its fierce looking fangs. Pink lotuses were in full bloom, impervious to the cold winter, and arranged in an orderly fashion along the border of the carpet. Flames from the burning logs danced merrily in the fireplace, making occasional hissing sounds.

Avinash carefully skirted around the dragon on the carpet and took a seat close to the fireplace.

'What I am going to disclose to you is highly confidential.' Speaking in a low voice, Lama Phunsok came up to Roy. 'Not a soul must know about it, not even your wife. Mr Roy, I…I need your professional help.'

'Professional help?' Roy couldn't help asking.

'Mr Roy, I am aware of who you are even though you have kept a low profile to avoid undue publicity.'

Roy stared back, his face giving away nothing.

'I know that you are a celebrated detective officer from Kolkata, highly regarded in police circles.'

Roy was both surprised and dismayed to learn that people

knew about him here.

'Don't be alarmed. I heard it from the Chief of Police.'

When Roy had requested the police department in Sikkim to arrange lodgings for him at Dengziang Monastery, he hadn't imagined it would reach the ears of the head lama. He suppressed a yawn, wishing Lama Phunsok would hurry up and come to the point.

'Care for some tea, Mr Roy? I have some traditional herbal teas that induce a good night's sleep.'

Meekly Roy nodded his head. How could he tell Lama Phunsok that he and his wife knew of a far more potent and enjoyable way of ensuring sound sleep at night?

Lama Phunsok seemed to be used to making his own tea. With practised ease, he poured water into the electric kettle, switched it on, took out a tin box, scooped out two spoonfuls of dark tea leaves and put them into the pot, and poured the boiling water into it. Tea was brought in exquisite blue porcelain cups, with lids to retain the heat. Roy took a sip. For a fleeting moment, he suspected he had been poisoned. It was the worst tea he had ever tasted—thick, buttery and pungent.

'It's not all that bad,' murmured Lama Phunsok, taken aback by the pained expression on Roy's face. 'Mr Roy,' suddenly his voice took an urgent, pleading note, 'please, please help me. I am… what you say in English…in dire trouble.'

Dire straits. Roy was about to correct the venerable lama, but didn't. He looked covertly at his wrist watch. It was past 11 p.m. Sharmi would be worried by now.

'Unless you tell me exactly what your trouble is, I can't help you.'

'You're right,' murmured Lama Phunsok. He walked with a painful gait across the carpet, unmindful of trampling upon the fire-spitting dragon. At length he drew a chair close to Roy and sat down, staring at the fireplace.

'Mr Roy, have you read the Bible? How much do you know about the missing years in Christ's life?'

Roy was plainly intrigued. Why should a Buddhist, monk in for away Sikkim, be worried about the missing years in Christ's life?

Lama Phunsok smiled briefly. 'I know what you're thinking. Why, as a Buddhist monk, should I bother about the missing chapter in Christ's life? Therein lies the mystery.'

Roy looked sharply at Lama Phunsok, but didn't say anything.

'It is said that twelve years in Christ's life cannot be traced. They are the missing years, supposedly spent in the Sinai deserts. What if I say a part of those years was actually spent in faraway India? In Kashmir, Benares, Nalanda and Puri?'

Roy looked gravely back at Lama Phunsok without saying a word.

'You think I am crazy, Mr Roy?'

Roy knitted his brows and tried to remember something.

'Many years ago I seemed to have read something of this kind somewhere. I forgot the details. But at that time the idea had seemed to be quite fanciful.'

'You actually meant preposterous, didn't you?'

A smile flickered momentarily on Roy's face.

'What if I tell you something even more preposterous? That Christ's rising from the dead wasn't only for the benefit of his disciples? That he lived long after that. He came down to India a second time, settled down in Kashmir and lived to a ripe old age. How about it? As a matter of fact, one can actually find his mortal remains at a place called Rozabaal, on the outskirts of old Srinagar.

Roy smiled and pondered for a moment. 'I'd say, it's even more fanciful.'

Lama Phunsok remained silent for a long moment, gazing at the fireplace. For a second, his eyes seemed to be ablaze, mirroring the flames.

'At times truth can be stranger than fiction.'

Roy remained silent, but all his attention was now riveted on Lama Phunsok.

'There's a rare Tibetan document written in Pali that bears a detailed account of Christ's life in India. It's difficult to say as to when it was actually written. Could be the second or third century. With the kind of scientific tools available now, you could perhaps ascertain its exact age.'

'Yes,' Roy stated sceptically. 'Provided, of course, such a document physically exists and is available for conducting such tests.'

The monk's face stiffened visibly.

'I am not given to hyperboles, or exaggeration, Mr Roy. If I say such a document exists, it exists. Because I have seen it myself, touched it, felt it between my fingers.'

'Good heavens!' Roy looked thoroughly alarmed. 'Don't tell me this document or manuscript, whatever you wish to call it, is actually here, in Dengziang Monastery?'

Lama Phunsok did not respond immediately. He walked across to the fireplace to put some fresh logs in it. He stoked the fire till it was blazing fiercely. When Lama Phunsok returned to his seat, his face, in spite of the physical exertions, looked visibly pale.

'Are you aware of the fact that by the end of the fifth century, the whole of Kashmir and Afghanistan had embraced Buddhism? And that the entire region was dotted with innumerable gumphas and Buddhist monasteries?'

Roy shook his head. He had never heard of it. 'What happened to them?'

'Either destroyed, or converted into mosques. The Bamian statue of Buddha...does that ring a bell?'

'Oh yes! Some 500-feet tall, wasn't it? The world's tallest statue of Buddha. Actually, carved out of a hill.'

'Yes. And destroyed by the Taliban in the most barbaric fashion. Such a pity! The statue was doing the Taliban no harm.' Lama Phunsok said with an audible sigh. 'But to come back to the point, the fourth World Buddhist Council took place in Kashmir in the year AD 78.'

'In Kashmir?' Roy looked blankly at Lama Phunsok.

The latter simply nodded his head.

'More importantly, in that congregation Christ was declared as one of the chosen ones in our religion. A living embodiment of the Avalokiteswara, the Buddha. You'll find it in the encyclopedia of Buddhist legends and doctrine, known as Mahavastu Avadana.'

Roy was absolutely speechless now. He just didn't know what to say.

'Have you ever been to Kashmir, Mr Roy? In which case you might also know that there is actually a mausoleum in a place called Khaniyar, at the outskirts of old Srinagar, which is zealously preserved and guarded by the local people as containing the mortal remains of Christ.'

A faint smile appeared on Phunsok's face as he watched Roy shake his head in sheer disbelief.

'Now perhaps you'll understand why Christ can be and is our concern. Because...he is one of us.'

Lama Phunsok carried on with steely conviction.

'This manuscript was originally preserved at Marbour, near Lhasa in Tibet. Later, a Tibetan version of the manuscript was brought over to Hemis Monastery in Ladakh.

'Because of the Chinese incursion?'

'No no, long before that, sometime during the seventh or eighth century. And please don't call it an incursion. It was an invasion. Let's call a spade a spade. The Chinese invasion of Tibet is one of the darkest chapters of twentieth century history. The whole world watched the Tibetans getting systematically decimated, their identity and religion trampled upon. And they did nothing. Absolutely nothing.'

Lama Phunsok kept quiet for sometime. It was clear that he was trying his level best to control himself. 'Anyway, what's the use of talking about all that now!'

'But why shift this manuscript from Ladakh to Sikkim?'

'Because Ladakh has become a very sensitive area now… not deemed safe anymore.'

Roy took a deep breath and shrugged elaborately. 'Well, I surely don't know what to make of this. This…is…incredible!'

'Mr Roy, officially the manuscript still exists in Ladakh, at Hemis Monastery.'

'Which means,' Roy's eyes widened as the full import of the truth dawned on him, 'nobody knows that this manuscript is actually here?'

'Exactly. Only a handful of people know about it. And now you do.'

For a long minute there was silence in the room, except for the logs burning in the fireplace.

'Okay, but why confide all this to me in the middle of the night?'

'Because…the manuscript is not here anymore. Gone. Missing.'

'What do you mean *missing*? You must have kept it hidden in a very secure place!'

'Yes, I did.'

'And hopefully nobody knows about it. At least nobody here!'

'That is true.'

'Are you sure it hasn't been misplaced by any chance? You know, memory can play strange tricks at times.'

Lama Phunsok shook his head.

'No no no... I've personally searched everywhere in the room. It's simply not there.'

The venerable monk leaned forward and held Roy's hand in his.

'I implore you, please find the manuscript for me. Or else, I am as good as dead.'

When Roy went back to his room, it was close to midnight. The entire monastery lay in silence. Not even an owl hooting. Only the sound of his footsteps echoing in the empty passage. Roy found the lights on in their bedroom. Poor Sharmi... was she still awake? Waiting for him? Like a thief he worked on the lock and tiptoed in.

Sharmi was fast asleep on the bed, curled up in a fetal position with just the shawl to keep her warm. Roy felt sorry for her. He remembered all the times in the past when he had returned home late and found Sharmi asleep, simply tired of waiting for him.

Careful so as not to wake her up, Roy took the blanket out from under the cover and gently spread it over Sharmi. A moment later the room went dark.

At this time of the year you could get a magnificent view of the sunrise over Kanchenjunga. The air is cold and crisp. No fog. No clouds. So, as the saying goes, on a clear day like this you could see forever.

Normally Avinash and Sharmi never tired of gazing at Kanchenjunga. If they spotted it in their walks, or while shopping, they would drop everything in hand and keep gazing at it hungrily. They could never have enough of it, while the locals went about their way, carrying sacks of potatoes and onions on their backs, oblivious of the towering presence of Kanchenjunga.

This morning, however, silence lay heavy between them. Neither of them even glanced at the splendid view of the peak outside.

This is what Avinash dreaded the most about Sharmi. She would carry on doing her daily chores without a murmur. But she would punish you by not speaking with you at all. There would be this stony silence about her that was impossible to breach. And this could go on for days, even weeks.

The first time this happened Avinash made all efforts to make up with her. He talked to her, coaxed her, cajoled her, even tried to make love to her. All to no avail. She would remain cold, frosty, unresponsive.

After that he just gave up. Let her take her time. If she didn't want to talk, it was fine by him. Not that he liked it. The entire thing was silly, even childish. But whoever said grownups don't behave childishly.

When they returned from breakfast, Sharmi couldn't contain herself anymore.

'If the lama has lost something he should have gone to the police. Why you?'

Roy had been pretty secretive about the whole thing, only

stating that something precious had been stolen from Lama Phunsok's possession.

'Fair enough, but why should he come rushing to you to solve his personal problems?'

'As I've already told you,' Roy said patiently, 'Lama Phunsok cannot go to the cops, for fear of the theft becoming public knowledge. The venerable lama would like to avoid this at all costs. It would ruin him professionally.'

'Let it ruin him, then. *Taate tomar ki?* Why should you care? He should have been far more careful, far more vigilant in the first place, if it's such a precious thing!'

'I think that's an uncharitable remark to make.'

'Uncharitable? Far from it. Actually, the problem is with you. At the faintest whiff of foul play, you charge at it like a bull terrier.'

'I didn't know,' Roy said with a faint smile, 'that I resemble a bull terrier in my pursuit of crime.'

'*Dhur chhai!* You are impossible.' Sharmi threw up her hands in frustration. 'What's the use of talking to you? You can't even remain serious for a minute.'

After lunch the private cab came at the appointed hour. Silently Avinash helped her with Sharmi luggage, ensuring that nothing had been left behind.

As the cab started, he drew back and waved at her. For a fleeting moment he thought Sharmi actually waved back at him, even if it was an infinitesimally small gesture.

Lama Phunsok took out a bunch of keys from the folds of his golden yellow and maroon robe and unlocked the heavy door.

'You wanted to see where our most valuable possessions are

kept secured, didn't you? So come along, Mr Roy.'

As the door creaked, Roy could see a flight of steps going down. The staircase looked dark and foreboding. After letting Roy in, Lama Phunsok bolted the latch from within.

'Just as a precaution...I don't want anyone else to know you're with me. Only senior lamas and their most trusted assistants have access to the underground vault. And that too, never alone. I handle the keys personally. At all times. There would be an absolute furore if anyone found out I have let you in.'

But Roy was hardly listening. At that time he was desperately trying to keep himself from panicking. How could he confess to Lama Phunsok that he suffered from claustrophobia? And that darkness only aggravated his problem?

Roy could hear Lama Phunsok pressing switches on the wall. A moment later the lights came on. Roy heaved a sigh of relief.

'As you can see...the electric cables on the wall are crude additions. They disfigure the beauty and symmetry of the monastery. Earlier times were much better. Oil torches in hand, we would tread down the steps.'

Frankly, Roy didn't fancy the earlier times at all.

'Talking of steps, you might want to watch it. They are steep and uneven, hewn from solid rock. Roy was painfully aware of that. In the dim light he had missed a step and had to desperately cling to the wall to regain his balance. On his bare fingers the effect was electric. Even in the afternoon the walls were frozen cold.

When they reached the base of the vault, Roy was pleasantly surprised. The place was much more brightly lit. He looked around, spellbound. He felt like Alice in Wonderland.

'I would never have imagined such a place exists deep in the bowels of a Buddhist monastery.'

A faint smile appeared on Lama Phunsok's face.

'There are so many things that you don't know about our monasteries.'

The place was simply dazzling. Gorgeous silk drapes hung down the wall, embroidered, possibly, with genuine gold threads. Majestic statues of Buddha lay in various positions of repose.

'Away from the public eye, this is where our most priceless possessions are preserved and guarded.'

'Meaning ancient manuscripts?'

'Not just that. Silver, gold, jewellery. Much more than you could ever imagine.'

'Gold and jewellery in a Buddhist monastery?' Roy's eyebrows were raised in enquiry. 'Where did they come from?'

'They were largely donated. Men in power, kings, rulers, potentates...when they converted to Buddhism they gave us money voluntarily, out of gratitude.'

'Out of gratitude? That sounds a little thin to me.'

'But true nevertheless. The kings and rulers who donated to us had done the same thing earlier. They had given away gold and jewellery to the temples. The practice of donation to Hindu gods and goddesses continues to this day.'

Roy had to nod his head.

'Why, I believe the wealth amassed in some of your temples would make oil magnates from the Middle East look like paupers in comparison.'

'But I thought Buddhism would be different. The true Buddhist is a 'vikhshyu', a beggar or mendicant, isn't it?'

'True. And we accepted these gifts as 'vikhshyus'. I cannot speak for other religions, but as Buddhist monks, we received these gifts because they were given out of gratitude. Not out of fear, nor coercion, nor with the threat of eternal damnation in hell if you do not tow a particular religious belief.'

'Er…revered lama,' Roy changed the subject. 'Could you show me exactly where this manuscript was kept?'

Lama Phunsok came to a section of the vault where the entire wall was covered by a giant wooden shelf, with hundreds of drawers in them.

'There.'

Lama Phunsok pointed out without hesitation, at the right hand corner, right near the ceiling.

'Third row from the top. Second on the right.'

'Any particular reason for keeping it up there?' Roy enquired.

'Yes…to keep it away from prying eyes.'

'The other drawers…do all of them have such manuscripts?'

'Yes. But none as precious as this one.'

'I see. You seemed to be so sure of where this manuscript is. Are you sure of all the other manuscripts?'

'Oh no! I do not have claims to any such miraculous power. I remember this particular document because I had to look for it again.'

'And why did you have to do that?' Roy gently enquired.

'That's the thing,' Lama Phunsok seemed to remember something in particular. 'You see…it's not every day that we visit the underground vault. We come here only on specific, auspicious days, based on our calendar. And then we inspect the treasures, just to make sure everything is okay.'

'When was the last time you conducted such an inspection?'

'Only four days ago.'

'So, what made you come back and recheck this manuscript in particular? Something that had struck you as odd perhaps? Only, the realization came later. And that's when you hastened back to the vault.'

'Exactly. But how did you…' Lama Phunsok left the question

unfinished and looked searchingly at Roy. 'I see...you are perceptive.'

Roy dismissed the compliment with a shrug and carried on.

'So what was it that had seemed odd to you?'

'The parchment on the cover page and the ink lettering—both seemed too fresh.'

'So you came back to verify the document again?'

'Yes. And to my infinite horror I found that the original manuscript had been replaced by a fake one.'

'A very clever piece of forgery. And perhaps it would have gone undetected ninety nine times out of hundred.'

Hands in pocket, for the room was getting quite cold even during day time, Roy paced around.

'Is anything else missing from the vault?'

'No, which is surprising, for there is a lot of jewellery here.'

'Are you a hundred percent sure of that?'

'Yes.'

'So, one can safely assume that whoever has made off with the manuscript came specifically for it.'

'I suppose so.'

Roy gave the woodwork a vigorous tug. But it didn't budge an inch. Obviously it was secured to the wall. He walked around different parts of the vault, tapping the wall all the time, listening for any hollow sound. There was none.

'I suppose there is no secret passage that comes down to this vault, is there?'

'None. I'm quite sure of it.'

'Hmm...interesting.' Roy stroked his chin thoughtfully.

'How many of you came down to the vault that day?'

'Let's see now,' Lama Phunsok tried to remember. 'There were two senior lamas other than me, and an assistant of mine. That's it, just the four of us.'

He looked intently at Roy.

'Why…you don't suspect anyone of my colleagues, do you?'

'Well,' Roy looked back directly at the lama. 'That's what you are going to tell me…who do you suspect?'

'Suspect?' Lama Phunsok was taken aback by the question. 'I don't know what you are driving at.'

'Come, come, sir. Don't you suspect anyone for this theft? Go back in your mind. Play back incidents of the last few days. Don't you find any anomaly anywhere? A false smile here or a furtive look there, perhaps on the face of one of your guests? Or one of the lamas here?'

The venerable lama thought for a while, then shook his head.

'Sorry, I don't…I can't suspect any of my colleagues.'

Roy remained silent for a moment.

'Is this out of a sense of loyalty that you are giving them a clean chit? Or, do you really not suspect anyone?'

Lama Phunsok looked resigned.

'I implicitly trust them. They've been with me in this monastery for years.'

'All right, I will rephrase the question.' Roy came and stood close to the lama. 'Do you have any enemies, then?'

A sad smile appeared on the face of the lama.

'Mr Roy, I know you are a man of the world. You certainly know this then. As a person goes up the ladder in the corporate world, he or she creates enemies.'

'But, we are not talking of a corporate world here. Yours is a sequestered world of prayers and meditations.'

'Small difference. The room at the top is not just lonely. It's also full of enemies, both in the corporate world and religious hierarchies.'

Roy shook his head. 'Lama Phunsok, you are talking in generalities. You need to be more specific, more frank. Otherwise I won't be able to help you.'

Lama Phunsok remained thoughtful for a while, perhaps trying to decide how much to confide in Roy. He cleared his throat and started talking.

'Earlier I had told you that only a very few knew of the existence of the manuscript here. Well, one of them is the Head Lama of Rhumtek Monastery in Gangtok.'

'How does he know about it?'

'When it was decided to shift the manuscript secretly from Hemis Monastery, the choice was between Rhumtek in Gangtok and Dengziang Monastery in Pelling.'

'I see,' Roy muttered to himself. 'The classic rivalry between two departmental heads over a prestigious product.'

'You've got the idea. Lama Tashi of Rhumtek Monastery was really hoping to get this manuscript from Hemis. Rhumtek, apart from being in the capital, is also the larger, more influential one in our hierarchy. So, if anyone found out that the prestigious manuscript is missing from Dengziang, I would be held personally responsible for it.' Lama Phunsok shook his head sadly. 'Worse, professionally I would be finished.'

'And, in the process, Lama Tashi would be earning some brownie points as well.'

'Brownie? I don't get it.'

'Sorry,' Roy smiled apologetically. 'What I meant was, in the process Lama Tashi would be strengthening his position in the hierarchy.'

'That is so.' It was clear that Phunsok wanted to avoid further discussion on the subject. 'Er…are we done here? Because I think we need to go back…don't want my absence noticed.'

'One last question, does this document have a name?'

'Not really. For our own convenience we call it the Issah Manuscript.'

'Why Issah?'

'In Kashmir Jesus was known by that name.'

The very next day, at the behest of Lama Phunsok, a team of electricians from NJP came and replaced the existing set of lights with LED bulbs, especially the compound lights. This measure was meant to bring economy to the monastery's general expenses.

Very few people knew that this was done at Roy's specific request. And only the venerable lama knew that the change in lighting was actually an elaborate cover for installing a covert CCTV surveillance system, manning all strategic points of the monastery. It included passages inside the guest house, staircases and even the entrance to the underground chamber.

'Miriam… Miss Miriam!' Roy called out to her. From the shadows of the first floor verandah he had observed Miriam leaving Dengziang Monastery that morning and had purposely allowed her a lead of about thirty steps before following her.

Miriam walked at a fast pace, her block heels clicking on the metalled road. Her swaying hips were discernible even through her unattractive sack-like garb. Roy wasn't a compulsive 'bird watcher'. But he found nothing wrong in appreciating an attractive lady as long as he didn't encroach her privacy or physically covet her.

Miriam stopped in her tracks and was evidently surprised to find Roy behind her.

'Miss Miriam, which way are you headed this morning?' Roy hastened to catch up with her.

'To the market. Why do you ask?'

'Excellent!' Roy clapped his hands in glee. 'Can I tag along with you, then? Oh no! Don't be alarmed. I am not stalking you. But maybe you could help me out with the purchase of a few provisions. I'm such a nincompoop in these matters.'

'That shouldn't be a problem. But first you have to tell me, where's your pretty wife? I don't see her with you.'

'Ah! What can I say Miss Miriam?' Roy rolled his eyes theatrically towards the heavens. 'In my old age she has deserted me. And now I have to fend for myself.'

'Poor you!' Miss Miriam said, a half-mocking smile playing on her lips. 'No problem, I will help you out with your purchases.'

As they walked towards the town Miriam plied him with myriad questions.

'The two of you were to vacate the monastery yesterday afternoon. So, what held you back?'

Roy gave her a disarming smile in answer. But secretly he thought, *Good heavens! Were they under such intense surveillance then?*

'Something of particular importance perhaps?' Miriam kept probing. 'Because everyone at the monastery thought the two of you were inseparable. And now to find you alone and so helpless…'

Was there a hint of flirtation in her voice now? This was surprising. Earlier Roy had found Miriam to be extremely shy and reserved, even to the point of being reticent. And now the new Miriam was so much more forthcoming, so much more free with him.

Did Sharmi's absence have something to do with it? Roy wondered. In her quiet unobtrusive way, Sharmi could be quite a formidable woman. There was something in her demeanour that, even when unspoken, clearly told other women to steer clear of her man.

'Is that what people think of us…inseparable?' Roy said in an amused voice.

'In fact, we have watched and envied you from a distance.'

'Is that so? How amusing!' He raised his eyebrows in enquiry.

Inwardly, however, his mind was racing. Miriam wasn't the mousy woman he had made her out to be. The eyes constantly downward cast, speaking ever so hesitantly—all this could be a neat façade, a rouge.

The whiff of sauciness in her voice plainly intrigued him. But what she had to say next shook him up even more.

'The grapevine has it that you are a sleuth from Kolkata with quite a formidable reputation. And that,' here she took a slight pause, 'your having to stay back has something to do with resolving some urgent issues.'

Roy's heart sank. How did this woman come to know all this? It was unthinkable that she had heard it from Lama Phunsok. Had the venerable lama confided about the theft to one or more of the senior lamas, then? And from there the words had reached the ears of Miriam?

Now, if that were so, Miriam could be close to one of the lamas out here. That was disturbing. It would have been so much easier for him if he could work on this case in complete anonymity.

'The beauty of a small town is…nothing remains secret here for long.'

Roy tried to make light of the whole thing. But Miriam kept on with her teasing banter.

'Tell me Mr Roy…is it something precious that's missing here? Or, have you stayed back to prevent an impending murder?'

'How prescient of you, Miriam! It actually might have something to do with a missing object. We are working on that. As for impending murder,' Roy's tone became more serious at this point, 'I wouldn't like to joke about it. Murder, after all, is a serious matter. Dead serious.'

'Now you are frightening me, Mr Roy!' Miriam exclaimed, her eyes widening for effect.

'Murder has a strange way of happening when you least expect it.' Roy said. Had he known how prophetic his words would turn out to be, he would have bitten his tongue to prevent himself saying so.

As they were rounding a bend a car came up from the opposite side and crossed them. As it passed by, he thought someone from inside was waving at them. But he couldn't be sure.

'That's surprising!' Roy slowed down his steps and kept looking behind. 'Did you notice someone waving at us from the car?'

'No I didn't.' Miriam shook her head. 'I wasn't watching.'

She looked up at him in amusement. 'Must be someone from Kolkata. Possibly one of your numerous female admirers.'

But Roy wasn't amused. He kept staring back at the receding car and tried to remember something.

'Come on, Mr Roy, you are seeing ghosts in every shadow now.' She took his hands in hers and resumed walking. 'Let's go. Or we'll be late.'

As she waltzed down the road she kept up with her merry chatter.

'Yours must be such an exciting career! Chasing spies and murderers and what not. When I was young I used to read Arthur Conan Doyle and instantly fell in love with Sherlock Holmes. Your life, I'm sure, is no less adventurous.'

'On the contrary,' Roy gently withdrew his hand from hers. 'It's so boring, it isn't even worth talking about. What about you, now? Is this your first time in Pelling?'

Roy knew very well it wasn't. But there was no harm in pretending ignorance.

'No, I've been coming here for the last five years. But didn't you know?'

'How could I, Miriam? It's my first visit here.'

'Oh, each year I come and stay here for about a month. I teach young lamas English and Maths.'

'In other words...you are corrupting them with your brand of western education.' Roy said in half-jest. 'Thousands of years of a unique culture, being destroyed in one fell move.'

'You don't mean that, do you?' Miriam didn't take his words lightly. 'Why should the lamas be denied education they deserve? Why should they not be allowed to catch up with the rest of the world? I know the concept of Shangri-La is so endearing to the western mind. A Utopia the world has never had. But that would be denying the Tibetans the right to a modern life.'

Roy could very well have argued back that they were not necessarily the best judges of what kind of life the Tibetans deserved. But he didn't.

'I suppose it's inevitable.' Roy sighed in reply. 'The onslaught of modern culture, it's all pervading. Why...only the other day I heard a young lama whistling the tune of a Hindi film song. So, Miriam...you are a teacher by profession?'

'Yes. Back in Coorg where I come from, I teach at a Jesuit Convent school.'

'How interesting! So, you come here for a month every year and teach the lamas. And I have a feeling that you don't charge a farthing for all this.'

Miriam nodded her head shyly.

'But why?'

'I know. People ask me this question all the time. They question my behaviour. They question why a young woman like me should spend her entire life like a monastic.'

'Does it mean that the opposite sex does not hold any attraction for you?' Roy said jokingly.

Miriam didn't provide any immediate answer. After a while she said, 'Can we sit somewhere for a while, Mr Roy?'

'You can call me Avinash.'

They found a culvert a little way ahead. A small mountain stream had gurgled down a moss-laden rock formation on the left side and ducked under the road to join a deep gorge on the other.

For a while they both sat in silence, watching the butterflies chase each other.

'Tell me, Avinash,' Miriam said in a low voice as she looked at the mountains.

'What is the secret of happiness?'

Roy just shrugged and smiled. He was adept at evading such 'profound' questions.

'Most of our lives we only think of ourselves. When something doesn't work out right, as it's bound to happen in life, we become acutely unhappy. The way out is to think beyond our petty selves. When I come here and teach the boys I'm filled with warmth. Perhaps you would call it the feel-good factor. That is the reward, Avinash. To me that represents happiness.'

When they reached the township, Miriam said, 'Avinash, I am sure accompanying me while I do the round of shops will bore you to death. So, why don't you give me your list of provisions and hang out somewhere else? Maybe have a cup of coffee or something?'

Roy didn't mind this arrangement. As a matter of fact, he needed a little time for himself to work out certain things in seclusion. Like having a word with Pradyot, his assistant in Kolkata. Sending some photos for identification; seeking background information on some of the people staying at Dengziang Monastery. All this would take a little time to accomplish.

At the appointed hour Roy waited at Café Terrace, just a few steps away from the main road. As he went up a short flight of steps from the road, he came upon the small restaurant filled with the aroma of freshly made garlic bread, croissants, sweet buns and doughnuts. There were a couple of tables inside the room, facing the glass showcase and the lone salesgirl at the counter. From this room, a green door led to the open terrace. Most of the tables and chairs were arranged outside, many of them fitted with colourful garden umbrellas.

Roy asked the salesgirl for a croissant and black coffee, paid at the counter and stepped out on the terrace. From there you could view a fair part of the sleepy township. The vegetable market, with tin roofs, painted green and red. To the left of the vegetable market and beyond the local post office were the open garment shops, with heaps of second-hand clothes—woollens and windcheaters laid out on the pavement. A little beyond the township the hills rose steeply, separated from each other by a considerable distance. But from there they looked sandwiched one upon the other. And beyond them, rising high up in the sky, was the towering presence of Kanchenjunga, now partially shrouded by a bank of clouds.

'Have you been waiting here for long?'

Roy turned around in surprise.

'Why Miriam…you look prettier than ever. Have you been running or something? Your cheeks look so flushed and pink!'

So, where had she rushed back from, that her cheeks had so much colour? Had she met her boyfriend just now? Had she visited his place before coming there? Was that why she had been so eager to get rid of him before doing her so-called shopping?

'A little brisk walk does you no harm,' Miriam said with a twinkle in her eye.

He took her to a table fitted with a large yellow and green and red umbrella. And there they had hot croissants with dollops of melting butter. The fresh aroma of the coffee sent them into a tizzy. As she held the cup in her left hand, Roy's eyes accidentally fell upon a pale white gash on her inner wrist. The mark on her fair skin was very faint. So if she had indeed slashed her own wrists it must have been long ago.

What could be the reason? Roy wondered. A love affair gone awry? Or, worse, a stepfather whose hands had groped all over her young body in the dark? The thought of it all made him depressed.

'What's the matter?' Miriam's grey-green eyes looked almost brown in the sun. 'All of a sudden you look so pensive and distant. Ah! I know. You must be missing your wife.'

Roy simply shook his head and looked away.

'Anyway, I've brought your provisions; biscuits, oats, marmalade. The local variety is pretty good, I can vouch for it... less synthetic stuff and all... so I brought you that and, let's see... oh yes, your green tea.'

Miriam handed over the provisions to Roy in a cloth bag.

'You don't have to return the bag. And here's the balance.'

Roy accepted the change and put it in his wallet.

'Where in Mangalore do you live?' He put a big chunk of croissant into his mouth and asked casually.

'Coorg, not Mangalore,' Miriam corrected him. 'And have you started interrogating me already?'

'About what?' Roy countered with a deadpan face.

'About whatever that is missing from Dengziang Monastery.'

Roy looked shrewdly at Miriam, but didn't say anything.

'Am I one of the suspects, Mr Roy?' she asked with a mischievous smile on her face.

'No, I don't think so. You are much too smart for that.'

'But do carry on with your questions. I find them so exciting!'

Just then two shadows crossed their table. Roy looked up for a moment to spot a couple of Lepchas sitting down at a table next to them. They had broad, flat faces and wide shoulders, and they spoke in a hushed tone. Just for a second, Roy's antennas were up. Then he relaxed. Maybe he was seeing ghosts in every passing shadow. Here was a lovely-looking woman by his side and a beautiful day to enjoy her company.

In any case, the two men seemed to be unaware of their presence and totally engrossed in conversing amongst themselves.

'Are you through with your coffee?' Roy looked at his watch and asked. 'At this rate we are going to miss our lunch at the monastery.'

But Miriam seemed to be in no hurry.

'Can we ask for something more?' Miriam pleaded with him. 'I just don't feel like going back to the monastery as yet. Anyway, lunch at the monastery is no great shakes,' she said, making a face. 'Let's stay back a little longer, please. It's such a lovely day. And I am enjoying your company.' She touched his arm lightly.

Roy got up and went inside. He looked at the stuff on the showcase, and then peeked from the green door.

'Is doughnut with honey all right with you...followed by a black forest?'

'That sounds heavenly!'

A little later Roy came back to the terrace with two trays in hand.

'The coffee's coming.'

The doughnuts were nice and soft and filling. So were the black forests. Roy and Miriam ate in a leisurely fashion and by the time they had finished their second cup of coffee, both of them looked sated.

'Thank you for a lovely lunch, Mr Roy... sorry, Avinash. Earlier I had planned to charge you for my services. But now I'm amply recompensed.'

The two of them got up quite happy and contented.

As they left the town behind, the road got steeper and steeper. Dengziang Monastery was at a considerably higher altitude than the township. On one side a steep hill tilted away from the road and, on the other, was the gorge, deepening, as you climbed up.

For a while both of them walked without a word. Coming down to the town was a lark. Returning to the monastery turned out to be a much more strenuous affair. On the way they passed the culvert where they had sat down earlier.

'You want to get your breath back, just let me know,' Miriam said, indicating the culvert. Roy was sorely tempted to sit down for a while and rest his tired feet. And yes, get his breath back. But male vanity somehow prevented him from doing so.

'I'm all right,' Roy said tersely, desperately hoping his heaving chest wasn't noticeable to her.

On the way back Miriam suddenly opened up. Maybe not so suddenly at that. Even on the terrace he had found her in a cheerful mood. Had she met up with someone just before, then? Someone she liked particularly? Did she have a boyfriend here? All this talk about not needing a man in order to be happy in life could just be an eyewash.

Anyway, Roy found her in an effusive mood. She confided in him as if she had known him for ages. She talked about her childhood. They were three sisters, she being the youngest and prettiest of the lot. She had been accidentally spotted by one of the nuns at Sunday church and been virtually adopted by the Christian missionaries. That had been the turning point in her life.

However, there was no mention of the attempted suicide. Was the experience still too raw in her memory to warrant a confession? Or was the pale white mark on her left wrist something else? Had he imagined the whole thing?

As he listened to her he seemed to hear a faint rumbling sound coming from somewhere. He couldn't quite place it. Suddenly, call it sixth sense, he looked up and found a huge chunk of rock hurtling down the hill. And it seemed to be coming straight upon them. There wasn't a single moment to lose. Roy just grabbed Miriam roughly and dived towards the side of the road. Had he been even a millisecond late, both of them would have been crushed to a pulp.

For a long moment they lay frozen, Miriam's body cocooned in Roy's arms. The boulder went hurtling past, missing them by inches. The entire ground rocked and rumbled as if there was a massive earthquake. Even as he closed his eyes in fear, he could hear trees getting squashed in the wake of the boulder as it sped down the gorge. Finally, there was the sound of a muffled explosion deep down below.

For more than a minute debris from above kept falling upon them—chipped stones, pebbles, chunks of muddy earth, tufts of grass—everything. And then…nothing. Just an eerie silence.

Gingerly Roy picked himself up and dusted himself. He stretched his limbs to make sure his body was still intact. He then held out a hand for Miriam. He noticed that the pupils of her eyes were dilated with fear. Her teeth were chattering. Gently, Roy wrapped his jacket around her and held her tightly.

'Tell me Mr Roy,' she whispered in his ears, 'this is for real, isn't it?'

Roy looked at the crater-like damage on the road and nodded his head imperceptively.

'I'm afraid so, Miriam.'

Pierre Duval was shaving in front of the bathroom mirror when he heard his cell phone ringing. He switched off the electric razor for a moment, to make sure. Yes, there it was; the distinctive tune of Für Elise that he had downloaded some time ago. One side of his face still lathered, he rushed to the bedroom to answer the phone.

'*Oui, c'est Pierre!*'

The voice from the other side was definitely French. But this being a remote hill station in Sikkim, the connection was pretty poor.

'*Allo... allo? Oui oui...*sorry can't hear you properly. Is it Martin?'

The voice from the other side was thick and guttural. Whatever Pierre could make out of the conversation, the voice was exhorting him to get out of the damn hotel room and come out in the open, so that they could have a proper conversation.

Pierre was about to hurry out of the room as he was, but stopped in mid-track. Merde! He fumbled around, then grabbed a towel, wrapped it around him, held the cell phone in the hollow between cheek and shoulder, opened the door and walked across to the far end of the verandah.

'Hello... *vous m'entendez*? Can you hear me now?'

'Of course I can hear you, you slimy bastard, now that you have unhitched yourself from that silly bitch.'

'No no... it's not like that. You are...'

The voice on the phone barked at him.

'Shut your fucking trap and listen to me. Pierre, you have been sent there for an important reason, not for whoring around. *Compre?*'

'*Oui oui...*I understand perfectly. Now if you will kindly compose yourself and let me explain... What? Don't shout like that, Martin. You are hurting my eardrums!'

Pierre was a smooth talker, if there ever was one. 'No no Martin, you've got it all wrong. Listen, there are people around. Someone might overhear!'

The voice on the phone came down a notch.

'So find a place where there are no people around, you stupid bastard.'

Pierre pretended not to hear this. 'Martin I really can't hear you.'

Pierre came down the steps quickly and moved away towards the back of the guest house. At last he found a place that was deserted.

'Okay, now we can talk.'

For the next ten minutes the voice on the phone spoke rapidly, without a pause. Whenever Pierre tried to interject, he was rudely asked to shut up. So, Pierre stood quietly, leaning against a wall, listening.

At length, Martin, or whoever it was on the phone, stopped speaking.

'Listen…trust me on this,' Pierre said in a confidential voice. 'We have to play it by the ear, you see. A slam-bang approach simply won't do. On the contrary, it might actually be counter-productive. So…no no no…I'm working on it…believe me.'

'All right,' the voice on the other side seemed to be a little pacified. 'I am giving you just one more week. 'Better get your act ready by then.'

The line went dead.

Pierre took a deep breath and then exhaled through his mouth, 'Pheeww!'

Even in this cold weather, sweat beads had appeared on his brow.

There was a knock on the door.

'Who's it?' Lama Phunsok enquired.

'It's me...Roy.'

'Oh! Please come in.' Lama Phunsok closed the book he was reading and hobbled across to the door to receive his guest. He escorted Roy to a comfortable chair and made him sit down.

'Any news for me, Mr Roy? I hope it's good.'

But one look at Roy's grave face and the enthusiasm in his voice died.

Roy was sorely tempted to curl his lips and snap back at him.

'Yah...news all right. But bloody bad news, thanks largely to you.'

Then he controlled himself and remained silent for a while. When he spoke it was in a quiet voice. But the note of seriousness made the lama sit up and take notice.

'I have somewhat disturbing news to share with you.'

'Yes?' Lama Phunsok looked at him attentively. 'Please tell me.'

'There's been a serious breach of trust and I'm afraid it's not on my part.'

'Breach of...sorry, I don't quite follow you.'

'You gave me to understand that the loss of the manuscript was to be kept totally a secret.'

'Yes, I did.' Lama Phunsok looked a little perplexed. 'So?'

'So...how does it become common knowledge in Dengziang Monastery? How does a lay person, not even one of your monks, tie up my staying back here with the loss of a priceless object? How does one get to know that I am a cop?' Roy stared hard at Lama Phunsok. 'Unless of course you've disclosed it to somebody else.'

Lama Phunsok looked aghast at Roy.

'I...I just don't...'

'Did you talk to anyone about this after you confided in me? Yes or no?'

'No, of course not. Do you think I am mad?' The lama answered angrily.

'Not even to one of your most senior lamas? Think…'

'There's nothing to think of. The answer is no.'

Roy was tempted to tell him that this disclosure had almost cost him and a woman their lives. There was absolutely no doubt in his mind that the afternoon's incident on the road wasn't an accident. It was an attempted murder. And almost flawlessly executed.

'I see.' Roy stared long and hard at the lama. 'Even the walls in Dengziang Monastery seem to have ears.'

That morning as the 12343 Darjeeling Mail rolled in at 8.15 a.m., New Jalpaiguri Station (NJP) presented a bedlam unusual for that hour. The reason was simple. It was the month of December. Parents were descending in hordes to fetch their children for the winter holidays. From NJP they would be taking private cabs to Darjeeling, Kalimpong, Kurseong or wherever their children's boarding schools were. If these schools charged you a bomb for teaching your kids how to get fashionably addicted to drugs, they at least had their name-dropping value. 'Oh! Your son's from North Point? That's fantastic.'

But, reality was drastically different. First, they made you bleed every month to meet your kids' whopping school fees. And, when they returned home with a 'dignified' pass, you paid another whopping sum of money to try and get him de-addicted from mandrak, or whichever drug was the flavour of the year.

Anyway, in a day's time these same men and women would be returning to NJP, turning the platforms into a potpourri of eager, young faces in blue and green blazers and grey flannel trousers and striped ties, displaying their school crests. In today's train there was also a smattering of foreigners who would like to take treks to Sandakphu from Darjeeling or spend a day in a toy train that chug-chugged its way in slow-mo, past Gorkha cottages at handshaking distance, and Indians who pretended they were used to a white Christmas. There were also a few die-hard Bengalis, wrapped in monkey-caps and comforters, their thermals showing through the dhotis, for whom it was de rigueur to travel to Darjeeling for Christmas.

The man who alighted last from the first class AC compartment of the Darjeeling Mail that morning wouldn't fit into any of these above categories. He was much too young to be one of the guardians. He didn't look like a regular tourist either. His eyes were much too disinterested, too cold. He could possibly be somewhere between thirty-five and forty, tall, wirily built, with close-cropped, curly hair. Had he only sported a moustache, he would've been taken for an army officer.

There was something about this man's demeanour that made you feel uncomfortable. Perhaps it was the way he brushed aside the coolies, as if they didn't exist. Or the dark glasses he wore so early in the morning, that made it impossible to make out what or whom he was staring at.

The man's baggage would indicate he was going to stay there for a while. He carried two strolley bags, one of them fairly large, and a shoulder bag. After coming out of the station, he had refused the coolie and carted the luggage himself. He stood apart from the rest of the crowd, the strolleys resting near his feet. All around him there was frenetic activity; passengers loading their luggage into cabs, haggling about the fare, street urchins on the lookout for a quick snatch job on any unaccompanied luggage.

In spite of wearing shades, he seemed to have made eye

contact with one of the private cab drivers who rushed forward to meet him.

'Where you be going, sir?'

'Pelling.'

'It would cost you 4,000 rupees, sir,' the driver said expectantly. He knew very well that, after haggling, the price would come down to 3,500, or, worst comes to worst, even to 3,200.

'Did I ask for the price?' the man said in an expressionless voice. The driver took one look at the man's face and shut up. As the driver bent down to pick up the luggage, the man roughly shoved him off.

'Leave it. I carry my own luggage.'

In the next four and a half hours the man didn't even once ask the driver to halt the car for tea, or anything else. They reached Pelling without a stop and, as a result, arrived half an hour early.

'Sir, I know good hotels. I take you there?' The driver directed the question through the rear view mirror.

'Nope, I have a booking at Hotel Kanchenjunga, near Dengziang Monastery. You know the place?'

'Yes, sir.'

'Then take me there.'

When they reached the hotel, the man paid the driver without a word, brought down the luggage all by himself and put them down at the hotel lobby. The driver of the taxi tarried a while, waiting. And when the hotel bellboy was rudely shoved away from the luggage, a faint smile appeared on his face. At least he wasn't the only one to receive that kind of treatment.

As for the man, he didn't take off his glasses even when he was signing the hotel register.

'Sir, we need guests to pay two days' tariff in advance.'

The clerk at the reception desk could feel the cold stare from behind those dark glasses. The man paid without a word.

'I need an east-facing room on the second floor.'

'Let me see, sir, if there is any vacant room...'

'There is nothing to see. I can see straightaway that all the keys of the second floor are in their keyholes.'

The clerk turned around, surprised.

'Why, so they are, sir.'

'I need to take a look at the room before checking in.

'Any particular requirement?'

The man sniggered back, 'Need to check if the toilet's functioning properly.'

The guest dragged the trolleys up the stairs—since there was no lift in the hotel—and waited for the bellboy to open the room for him. He cast a cursory glance at the toilet before coming back to the bedroom. He looked through the curtains casually and nodded to himself.

'Inform at the reception that I will take this room.' He tipped the bellboy, waiting for him to leave, then locked the room from inside. He stood still for a moment in the centre of the room, doing nothing.

He then decided to hoist the larger of the trolley bags on the bed, apparently without effort, and unlocked it. Systematically, he started taking out item after item from the suitcase and arranged them neatly on the bed. From an odd-shaped box came out a pair of knives, one of them fitted with a hidden spring mechanism. As the guest pressed a small button on the handle, the sharp end of the knife sprang open. With a practised motion he went on to close it with the palm of his hand and placed it on the bed. The other knife was different—its broad blade thick on one side and razor-sharp on the other. He carefully felt the sharpness of the blade with the tip of his finger, then sheathed it back inside the case. From a rectangular-shaped container came out a camera, fitted with a powerful tele-lens; then a binocular, a length of nylon ropes, a pair of black leather gloves, a small bore revolver, and then, a long, flat rectangular box, with a zip all around. Upon opening, it revealed an 18-inch steel tube, a dark, compact butt and several other components. As the stranger assembled them, it turned out to be a telescopic rifle.

At last he took off his sunglasses, and one would see with relief that he wasn't partially blind or anything. He shifted the drawn curtain of the east-facing window just a little bit and looked out. From the second floor room it gave the man a pretty good view of not just the Dengziang Monastery but also that of the two-storied guest house. Taking the binoculars from the bed, the stranger trained it on the first floor of the guest house. Just then one of the guest rooms opened its doors and a man came out. The stranger focused on the face of this man and one could make out it was Roy. The stranger shifted focus to the number on the door of the room. It read 106.

For the first time since the morning a thin smile appeared on his face. He drew the curtains back, picked up the small bore revolver and the flick-knife from the bed, put on the dark glasses that made his eyes invisible once again and left the room.

Needless to say, on his way out he did not leave the keys with the reception.

Miriam gently eased her body into the bathtub. The water felt warm against her skin. She lay still for a moment, deep in thought. But actually there wasn't much to think about. The decision had already been taken. She had been waiting for this day for some time—waiting for the house to be vacant so that she could execute her plan.

Mom had gone for work. She ran a boutique for women. Her elder sisters were in school. Miriam was also supposed to have gone to school with them. But she had pleaded to be allowed to stay home, citing a splitting headache as her excuse. Mom didn't bother too much about it. Dad was away on one of his business trips. He would be back only that evening. By then everything would be over. As for her maternal uncle, he had gone to Coorg to settle some long-pending land deal.

Miriam knew this had to be her day. There was nothing to hurry about, though. She had the whole day in front of her. She coolly walked to the kitchen, opened the drawer that stored all the knives. After careful inspection she selected the vegetable chopper, its broad blade, sharp and glistening. Then she took out a fresh towel from the cupboard, wrapped it around the knife and padded back to the bathroom.

Already the water in the bathtub was more than half full, and rising. She leaned forward to test the water with her fingertips. The temperature seemed to be just right. She placed the knife on a wooden stool conveniently close to the bathtub, then stood up and looked into the mirror. For a while her grey-green eyes surveyed her own face, as if staring at a stranger.

'Miriam,' she whispered to herself, 'do you really want to go ahead with it?'

She took time to consider the question, then quietly nodded. She smiled to herself, a last tentative smile. Then she let the dressing gown fall on the floor. Now she was naked. She studied her breasts in the mirror. They were still growing. The lighter areolae, culminating in the darker-shaded teats, protruded from her breasts like twin golden-brown grapes. She cupped her breasts with her hands for a while, studying them closely, then let go of her hands. The breasts didn't sag one bit. She sighed softly to herself, looking at her own pale face, fully aware of the consequences of her decision.

Abruptly, she left the mirror and stepped into the bathtub. By now the line of water had swollen to her breasts, making them float. Eyes closed, she lay still in the water, thinking. But actually, there wasn't much to think about. The decision had already been taken. Did she feel sorry for herself? No. Did she feel sorry for anybody else, then? Yes, probably her father. He loved her unconditionally. Maybe she felt sorry for Julia, her eldest sister. Julia was like a mother to her.

Miriam stretched her right hand and reached out for the vegetable chopper on the wooden stool. Then she placed her left wrist on the curvature of the tub and brought the chopper down. Diagonally across her wrist. Not with too much force though. You don't need to chop your entire hand off to kill yourself. She watched blood spurt out from her veins in thick scarlet blobs. She put the chopper back on the wooden stool and sank back into the water. Blood spread across the bathtub like billowing, red clouds.

Strangely, Miriam didn't feel any pain. She watched life gently ooze out through her left wrist. Everything was so calm, so serene. She had drawn the curtains aside beforehand, so she could see a patch of blue through the window. Gradually, the blue in the sky faded into grey, the twittering of the birds receded into the distance. Finally, all was silent.

Julia kept screaming, shrieking and howling till somebody slapped her hard on the face. Her body sagged down on the floor and she started moaning softly. You couldn't blame her for behaving like this. She was the first to spot Miriam in the bathtub.

There was blood everywhere—overflowing from the bathtub, staining the tiled floor a deep scarlet, coursing down in a tiny rivulet to the outlet at the far end of the bathroom.

As Dr Rao would recount later innumerable times, the survival of Miriam was a miracle three times over.

The first miracle was Julia's returning home early that day because of acute stomach cramps. It happened to be the first day of her menstrual cycle. The second miracle was the fact that Miriam didn't drown in the bathtub. In such a situation many people did. And the third miracle was that the gash hadn't penetrated the radial artery. Had it done so, she would have been dead in less than half an hour.

Even then, her life hung in the balance for a long time. In the absence of a rubber tube to tie up and stem the flow of blood from the wound, Dr Rao had used his presence of mind to wrap the blood pressure apparatus tightly around her arm and pump air into it to choke off the wound. He had lifted Miriam's inert body in his arms, ran across to his car, put her down gently on the rear seats and then raced his car to the hospital. He had called the hospital up while still driving, a thing that he would never do in his senses, so that there were people to take charge of her as soon as he reached the hospital.

When Miriam finally returned home after recovery she had become a ghost of her former self. Her eyes had sunken deep. Her complexion had turned grey, like old parchment paper. What was worse, she behaved like a zombie. It seemed that she had lost the ability to do anything on her own. She had to be brushed, bathed, clothed and fed by her sisters. She slept very little. And when she did, she kept waking up screaming in the middle of the night, as if watching a horror movie on a loop.

Often she would stare, terrified, at the door, as if dreading someone's visit. And then, without any cause, she would put up her frail hands in self-defense and plead to an imaginary person, crying, 'Please don't, please...' Then, she would whimper and cry, as though in immense pain.

At such times, her father, a giant of a man, would cradle her in his arms, rocking to and fro, whispering all the time that the demons had been exorcised for all times to come; that they would never bother her again. It was rumoured that on the night of her attempted suicide, when Raju, the maternal uncle, had finally returned home, Miriam's father had literally lifted him from the floor and shook him up so violently that the poor man had peed in his pants. Raju uncle had disappeared from the house that very night and was never to be seen again. The doctors at the hospital had confirmed that Miriam had been violated, not once, but repeatedly, over a period of time.

The turning point in her life was probably the visit of Sister Cybil, from her school. She would come regularly in the evenings and sit down by her side, simply holding her hands. Most of the times she didn't speak at all. There was just this comfortable silence between the two of them. One day, Miriam got up from her sleep with a smile and was normal again. Just like that. But her mind had been made up. She wasn't going to stay home anymore. No amount of coaxing and cajoling on the part of the mother or the sisters could change her mind.

Miriam shifted to the hostel of the school she was studying in. The sisters and nuns at the school were, of course, overjoyed. She wasn't just a devout Christian (invariably she earned the highest marks in Catechism in her class), with her recent traumatic past, she was just the right material for joining sisterhood. But they didn't want to push her into it. As Mother Superior would fondly remark, 'She is so young a creature, still virtually a child.' The fervour with which she would kneel down before the church altar and recite *Ave Maria gratias plena* would move Mother Superior to tears.

Two years after completing secular studies, she was accepted by the church for candidacy. It involved one year of initial training, during which she was required to study the Bible in greater depth and spend more and more time in meditation. 'Don't be dismayed if your mind wavers and you find yourself thinking of something else.' Mother Superior would tell the novices. 'It happens with all of us. In such a situation all you need to do is relax and allow those thoughts to pass through your mind. Gradually you will be able to empty your mind and meditate.'

After three years she was allowed to take her first vows— chastity, poverty, obedience. Though she had been violated repeatedly, in the heart of her heart she felt she was still chaste.

'Poverty doesn't mean you have to live in rags and eat leftovers,' Mother Superior assured the novices. 'It simply means that you cultivate an indifference towards worldly goods; accept what comes to you as God's gift and not grumble about it. As for obedience, I don't think I have to explain it to you. You have to have implicit obedience to the church, to the Bible, to your seniors. That's it. Quite simple, isn't it?' Mother was relieved to find that her novices had taken it well. The vows could seem to be quite daunting initially.

That morning there was absolute chaos in Dengziang. A minivan and two SUVs, loaded with camera, lights, stands, reflectors, recording equipment and miles and miles of coiled wire, came in through the front gate and parked themselves on the courtyard facing the entrance of the monastery. The sentry at the gate was so stupefied he couldn't even ask where they were from. The babel of alien languages, spoken in high decibel, shattered the morning calmness of the monastery.

Lama Phunsok came out, looking absolutely aghast. Who were these people? Where had they arrived from? What were they doing here?

Upon questioning, the film crew had taken Pierre Duval's name. The Frenchman was immediately summoned.

'But revered lama,' Pierre promptly produced a typed piece of paper, signed by the lama himself, 'you have agreed in writing to let me shoot a documentary here.'

Lama Phunsok peered at the document. It was a letter from Pierre to the authorities in Dengziang seeking permission to shoot a documentary. At the bottom of the letter the senior lama had, indeed, signed his approval.

'But when I gave you the approval I had no idea it would turn out to be such an elaborate affair.' He shook his head in dismay. He knew he had been caught in a bind.

'No matter,' Pierre said magnanimously. 'I will arrange for the crew to stay elsewhere. But, during daytime we have to shoot here and they have to be here.'

'With all this chatter and noise?'

'No no…this is just because we're unloading the equipment. Once they settle down we would remain as quiet as a graveyard. Trust me.' The lama kept quiet. But inside he was fuming. It was very doubtful if he would ever trust Pierre again. Once the film was ready, it would be marketed worldwide. Pierre could end up making a fortune. And what would the monastery get in return? Nothing.

'But Lama Phunsok,' Pierre seemed to sense the resentment in the lama, 'Dengziang would become internationally famous overnight. People would come from all over the world to see this marvellous monastery. Think of all the added footfalls.'

'I'm dreading it already,' muttered the lama.

Roy had gone out in the morning for a walk. When he returned he was dismayed to see Duval's unit unloading equipment at the monastery. He had fondly hoped that Duval's 'documentary maker' tag was only a cover. He had some other, more sinister motive for hanging around there. But now he was proved wrong.

As he collected the keys from the desk and was crossing the courtyard, he observed another bunch of people working in the compound. He stopped and watched them set up new lights in place of the existing ones. After a while, a faint smile appeared on his face and he went up the stairs whistling a merry tune.

The first time that Miriam had come to Pelling was on a friend's recommendation. Her friend had said, 'Forget the Nilgiris. If you like the mountains, visit Sikkim. Much of it is still unspoilt, still very beautiful. And you'll find solitude there.'

So she had visited Sikkim, doing the usual touristy rounds, Gangtok first and thereafter, to Rhumtek. After all, Sikkim abounds in Buddhist monasteries. From there, up the mountains, to Chhangu Lake, Nathula Pass. And then she travelled back to Gangtok, proceeding to Pelling, visiting the Khechupuri Lake, Dengziang Monastery, the Rabdantse ruins.

The first time she hadn't intended to stay at Dengziang for more than an hour. But a sudden shower had forced her to take shelter at the dormitory of the little lamas. And there they were—kids barely five years old, heads shaven, plump pink cheeks, laughing and giggling all the time—she just fell in love with them.

Next year she came back to Sikkim, she headed straight for Pelling. Upon enquiry she found out that there was a guest house within the compounds of the monastery. She could stay there if she taught the children. No problem, she said. She happened to be a school teacher in real life. The kids wished to learn Maths and English. Indeed, they already had a German lady who came and taught there for a month every year. But, this lady's English wasn't too good. And she spoke no Hindi, which was a big drawback. Miriam immediately offered her own services. She spoke Hindi well. And her English was better. It was, after all, her mother tongue. And she was very good at Maths. So, would they consider her as one of their teachers? Why not? came the reply.

The very next day she moved into the monastery guest house. Thus began her time with the little kids. She simply loved their simplicity, their open-heartedness. Of course, the liking was mutual. In no time at all, she became the most popular teacher in the monastery.

Miriam felt happy. Perhaps this was the happiest period of her life. To be wanted, to be loved by these kids. When it was time for her to return to Coorg, the children literally cried and begged her to stay back.

She left, with a promise to come back. And she did. Next year, same time, she returned to the monastery. The kids were beside themselves with joy. They formed a circle around her and did an improvised jig in celebration of her return. On weekends they would often take her to their homes. The little lamas were allowed to go home once a week. And the one that she was most fond of was Tenzing. He came from a Lepcha family that stayed right in the heart of the township. He had an elder brother, named Johnny, who was older than him by ten years.

Now, Johnny wasn't his actual name. His Lepcha name, Yun song Choi, was so unpronounceable to the average tourist that he had to adopt a different, easier name for himself. You see, Johnny was a tourist guide-cum-taxi driver by profession. So it was important that people remembered his name without trying.

He was also a bit of a clown and an entertainer. He would cook up funny stories about himself all the time, knowing well that his customers wouldn't believe him. So what? He always managed to raise a laugh, which was pretty good for business. You are paying for the cab and getting the entertainment for free. Now, who wouldn't want that?

The first time Miriam came over to Tenzing and Johnny's home, their mother gave her a traditional Lepcha welcome, wrapping a silk scarf around her neck. They made her sit at the dining table, the only furniture in the room, and offered her hot pork momos and garlic soup. When it was time for her to return to the monastery, Johnny insisted on dropping her in his own cab. And he refused to take any money for it.

'You are my brother's teacher. How can I accept money from you?'

The first year that Miriam taught at the monastery, Tenzing was just a small boy. But last year Miriam had suddenly found him growing up into a big fellow. This was strange, because his elder brother Johnny was short and lean in stature. And this year she could scarcely recognize him, he had become so huge. At fifteen, Tenzing had grown up into a man. This should hardly have been a matter of discomfiture for her. But it was. His physical proximity made her feel terribly uncomfortable and clumsy. In trying to flip through the pages, she would drop the textbook from her hand; in an attempt to take the ball pen out she would scatter the contents of her entire handbag all over the floor. Was it actually nervousness or an excuse for her to allow Tenzing to come and pick up the stuff for her? And in doing so, his hands would inevitably brush against hers. Was that what she really wanted?

The other day as she left her class and was going down the steps, she inexplicably fell down and twisted her ankle. And she almost fainted when Tenzing swooped down upon her and picked her up in his arms as if she was just a child. With her face against his chest, she could actually hear his heartbeat. Was that why she had really fallen down?

In the afternoon Roy made coffee for himself and sat down to do some serious thinking. Wherever he travelled, he carried with him, no, not an electric kettle—it was much too cumbersome to handle—but a tiny immersion heater and a stainless steel mug with

a bakelite handle. Though the notice pinned on the reverse side
of the door expressly prohibited the use of any electrical gadgets,
other than shavers and hair dryers, he chose to ignore it. He drank
gallons of tea and coffee every day and simply couldn't be bothered
about complying with such silly orders. The coffee, given to him by
his son on his last trip to Kolkata, was unbranded. Made of virgin
South Colombian beans, it filled the room with a heavenly aroma.

He took the coffee to the balcony and leaned against the railing.
Downstairs Duval's film crew was busy arranging camera stands,
lights and all the other paraphernalia involved in a film shoot. As
he idly watched their proceedings, his mind was busy playing back
the incident of the afternoon. The boulder thing couldn't have been
an accident. Not by a long shot. Huge boulders do not roll down
the hill of their own accord. It would require a major earthquake
or a landslide to dislodge such a heavy object. But there had been
no earthquakes, no landslides that day. And for that matter, why
should the boulder come hurtling down precisely when they were
passing by on the road? Roy didn't believe in coincidences.

Now, if it was a deliberate attempt to murder, who was it aimed
at? Him? Or Miriam? Or was it a bold attempt to do away with
both of them in one fell swoop? He shrugged. He didn't know.
But by devil, he would, and sooner than later. Now, if he didn't
know the *who*, there was always the *why*. Why should anyone
want to kill him, or Miriam? Because Roy had stayed back to try
and retrieve the missing Issah manuscript? This meant, there were
powerful elements in Pelling that didn't want him to proceed with
the investigation. As simple as that.

And Miriam? How was she involved in all this? Why should
anyone want to liquidate her? Just because she knew about the
theft? Or because she was actually a part of it? Could there be a
rival gang that wanted her out of the way, permanently? Or was

there a sex angle to the whole thing? Never mind her touch-me-not frostiness, could she be secretly having an affair with someone out there? If so, who with? One of the guests? Or one of the lamas? Surely lamas could also fall prey to the charms of the opposite sex? A faint smile appeared on his face. The whole thing was getting quite interesting.

Downstairs, the camera and the crew had taken shots of the exterior of the monastery. The men were now moving into the dormitory of the novitiate lamas. Roy drained the remaining coffee in one gulp and went inside to pour some more for himself from the thermos. This time he sat down on one of the cane chairs and put his feet up on the railing.

Those intending to kill him or her would be persons interested in getting hold of the manuscript, right? Then who were the obvious suspects behind the theft?

Let's take William 'Billy' Ford first. What did one know about him? Nothing, except the publicized fact that he was there to collect rare tankhas and Tara figurines. Was he actually hoping to bribe his way through the officials there and make off with the stuff? Otherwise, it didn't make sense for him to stay there all this time.

Roy scratched his chin, thinking. He had forgotten to shave that morning.

But it would be a darned difficult task to carry out. The tankhas at Dengziang Monastery were pretty large in size and the bronze Tara figurines quite heavy. Not the easiest objects to take away in front of so many people. So, perhaps Billy had something else up his sleeve, and this being a 'collector' of objects of art was only a cover. But what was his real motive for hanging out there then? Was he also in the race for the Issah manuscript?

On the face of it it seemed rather unlikely, reasoned Roy.

Miriam had most possibly learnt about the theft through one of her contacts amongst the lamas, not the foreign guests in the monastery. So, Billy's real reason for staying there still remained a mystery.

Next amongst the suspects was Duval. Right from the outset Roy had never been quite comfortable with him. He had suspected him of using this 'docu maker' tag as a front. Roy wondered what Duval was really up to. Could he actually be using the whole filmmaking thing as an elaborate cover for something far more sinister? If so, what? The Issah papers? Or was Duval a pedophile? So, while his filmmaking thing could be genuine, he would be able to carry on having his little bit of fun on the side with the lamas.

So what's the conclusion? While his involvement in the Issah document was inconclusive, his movements needed to be carefully monitored.

Last in the list of suspects, as far as the outsiders were concerned, was the 'mousy' couple. Roy didn't know anything about them, which country they were from, their reason for being there...nothing. Were they there simply as tourists? But then, they hadn't taken any of the popular sightseeing trips undertaken by tourists there. Not even once. They were always leaving the monastery for these long, mysterious little trips to Pelling, and from there, to one of the small villages nearby. Most days, they skipped lunch. Sometimes they would return only late in the evening. What did they do in the village? This was an area certainly worth looking at.

Amidst all this uncertainty Roy was sure of only two things. One, there was a definite link between this afternoon's murder attempt on them and the stolen manuscript. Two, the theft could not possibly have taken place without inside help. So, one or more of the lamas in the monastery had to be involved.

His mind kept going back to the fateful evening when Lama Phunsok had made his disclosure to him. How could anyone else have got wind of it? He played back the entire evening's incidents in his mind, from the moment of Lama Tenzing's coming over to call him to the time of his retiring to his room. Had someone been eavesdropping on them while they were in Phunsok's room?

Just then somebody cleared his throat behind him and said, 'Avinash Roy I presume.'

Roy had been so engrossed in thought that it hadn't even occurred to him that someone could actually sneak up from behind to the first floor balcony of the guest house. Who could it be? The voice sounded familiar. He willed himself to turn around slowly and confront the stranger. To his great surprise and relief it turned out to be none other than Pradyot, his assistant from Kolkata. With the French cut beard and the large dark sunglasses, he seemed almost unrecognizable.

A couple of days after Sharmi had left, Roy chose to share Billy's table at breakfast.

'Welcome, buddy,' Billy boomed in his baritone, making room for Roy. As usual, Roy cringed at the thought of drawing attention in the dining hall.

'So, you too have become a lone wolf, like the rest of us.'

Roy resented the comparison. 'Us' in Billy's lexicon would, in all likelihood, comprise Duval and himself.

'How did you get rid of your wife, buddy boy? Threw her down a precipice? Or is it something more mundane, like packing her off home?

Roy wore his smile like a mask.

'Buddy, you can't deceive an old horse like me. Men are all alike. When the cat's away, the mice will play. So, which pretty skirt are you chasing this time? I know, it has to be Miriam.'

'Bravo, Billy, you are the wit this morning,' Roy's voice was dripping with sarcasm. But Billy was dense enough to take it as a compliment.

Roy was saved further discomfiture with the arrival of breakfast. It contained a generous platter of dark brown, succulent pork sausages, followed by crisply fried bacon and eggs on toast.

Billy looked down at the plates with pleasure. 'Hate fruit juice, man, especially if it's canned.'

It was easy to see that Billy had asked for special breakfast that morning. The normal breakfast served at Dengziang consisted of a frugal bowl of porridge, a couple of toasts and, if you were very lucky, a boiled egg.

As the bearer reappeared at the table with a large pot of coffee, Billy ordered some more breakfast for Roy. When it arrived, Roy ate with guilty pleasure. Sharmi wasn't around. No one was going to tick him off for indulging in pork sausages and fried bacon, both items high in cholesterol.

'So, what kept you back, Roy?' Billy asked, as he licked the yolk dripping from his fingertips.

'You.'

'Wha…what?' Billy almost choked on his coffee.

'You and Duval and all the other phirangs that frequent this place without apparently having anything to do.' The manner of speaking might have sounded flippant. But the intent, certainly, wasn't.

'What are you doing here Billy?' Roy said, leaning across the table. 'Who are you hiding from in the States? You've been here more than a month. I've checked. And you've got nothing to show for it. Your being a collector of objects of art is a lot of hogwash. Is it the law, Billy? Or, is it your wife?'

'What do you mean? I am an art collector.'

'Where's your collection, Billy?' He carried on. 'I might want to take a look at it.'

Suddenly, Billy was no more his usual blustering self anymore.

'Hey buddy, we're still pals…remember?' His voice had taken a more conciliatory tone now. 'Sure, I'll show you my collection, if you're really keen to see it.'

'Are we talking of genuinely old art objects? Or junk, fake stuff, artificially aged, to make it look like the real thing?'

'Hey, hey, buddy,' Billy took a quick look around to see if anyone was listening. 'It's not like that at all. Not what you think.'

'How do you know what I'm thinking? Right now what I am thinking, Billy buddy boy, is you are a fugitive from justice. And the passport that you are carrying right now might very well be a fake one.'

Roy took a sip of coffee and looked steadily at Billy.

'How did you make it to India, buddy boy? Did you come via Kenya? Or was it Nigeria? What stuff did you smuggle in from there? Cocaine? Or designer, synthetic drugs? I want to know all about that Billy, I really do.'

By this time Roy had brought forward his face to a whispering distance.

'Drink up your coffee, man,' Roy said, deliberately mimicking a black American accent. 'Your coffee's got sorta cold.'

By now Billy was looking thoroughly alarmed.

'You got it all wrong, Roy,' he said in explanation.' My passport and visa, they are all legit, I promise. And why should I come via Kenya or Nigeria? I don't do drugs, man. Believe me.'

'I believe you, Billy buddy boy,' Roy's voice relaxed a little. 'I was just pulling your leg.'

For a moment, the big American was speechless.

'Phew!' he blew air out through his mouth. 'For a while you had me scared…really scared.' He clipped Roy hard on the shoulder in sheer relief. 'But, you're a shrewd bastard, I'll grant you that. I did actually run away from the US. But not from the law. It's my wife, man. She's a viper, a vicious snake. She doesn't even know I'm in India, in Pelling. Or she might come chasing me down all the way from Alabama.'

'If she's really what you profess her to be, why did you get hitched to her in the first place?' Roy asked innocently.

'How would I know, man? When I first met her, she was sweet as honey. So cute, so lovable she was.' Billy had a misty, faraway look in his eyes. 'But she was a cock-teaser all right. She wouldn't let me touch her. A kiss was all that I was allowed, nothing more. She wouldn't let me touch her breasts, feel up her butter-soft buttocks. Man, just seeing her made me so wild and horny, like I'd never been in my life. So finally I get married to her. And then the real fun started.'

At this point Billy stopped his narrative abruptly. But Roy's appetite had been whetted by now.

'What do you mean…real fun?'

'It's the classic tragedy, man. I went to bed with a virgin. And I woke up with a nymphomaniac. Actually I didn't sleep that night at all. Nor the next. Or the next. Within a week I had become half of myself, man. Totally exhausted, drained, pooped. She was sucking the life out of me. Night after night. Like a vampire. Within a month I had become like a skeleton. At the office I could hardly keep my eyes open. So, I told her. I wanted to sleep at least four hours at night to stay alive. But she would have none of it. I tried to sleep in the guest room. But in the middle of the night she started banging the door loudly. Till all my neighbours woke up and started hollering. So, out of sheer awkwardness, I opened the room. And you know what she does then?'

Here, Billy took a dramatic pause. 'She just trips me down and comes on top of me right on the floor. She starts riding me like she was a cowboy. Okay. So, we come off together. Boom! Fantastic! But then, within five minutes she's hot again. But, I can't, see…I'm human. So, she takes me in her hands and fondles me ever so softly, and then suddenly she puts me in her mouth and nibbles at me. Ouch! I almost jump out of my own skin. But, magically, I'm hard again. So, she jumps on top of me again and encircles me with her legs. Oh god! It feels great, gorgeous! But, you can't keep it up for long, not every half an hour. But you know, the funny thing was she said she loved me. And she wouldn't have sex with anybody else. Man,' Billy looked pleadingly at me, 'how could I take that anymore? I thought I was born with high libido. She cured me of that. Today, even the thought of sex makes me want to puke.'

Billy finally stopped and took a deep breath. The dining hall had become empty by now. A couple of waiters hovered around to clear the table. They came out of the dining room and climbed up the stairs to the balcony.

'Mind if I smoke?' Billy asked.

Roy shook his head. 'It's your pair of lungs, buddy, not mine.'

Billy sat a little distance from Roy and put his long legs up on the railing and lit a fat cigar.

'Care for one, pal?' he extended a leather case full of cigars. 'They are Havanas.'

'Nope.' Roy shook his head.

For a while both men remained silent. The aroma of Havana

cigar spread across the balcony.

'I only have a couple of them a day, mainly after meals. But today I feel like having one now. Perhaps it's because of all the talking I've done.'

'But Billy,' Roy squinted against the bright sky, 'you still haven't told me what you do for a living. You've been here for more than a month now. Where's the money coming from? Your dad owns Fort Knox, or what?'

'Gas, man,' Billy creased his face in a grin and puffed away. 'Our family owns a chain of gas stations, all over Alabama.'

Suddenly, there was commotion downstairs. Roy got up to take a look. Apparently a tourist had fainted.

'Busy?' Roy stood at the half open door and asked. Inside, Lama Chorten was tidying up his room.

'No no, do come in.'

Roy had visited Chorten a couple of times before, while Sharmi was there. There was an air of calm serenity about the young lama that belied his age. It had instinctively drawn Roy towards him. Chorten had shortly completed his apprenticeship and had become a full-fledged lama. It allowed him the privacy of his own room. Even a few days ago he had been sharing the dormitory with the other trainee lamas.

'Anything the matter?'

Roy shook his head.

'I just had a little time to myself and thought why not come and visit you.'

'Want to sit down?' Chorten spread a couple of square mattresses on the floor. The room was small. It had just one window. The young lamas, as well as lamas in training, shared common toilets.

'No, thanks!' Roy went to the window and looked out. Outside, there were a couple of squash trees, their branches so heavily laden with fruit that they almost touched the ground. There was also a solitary rhododendron tree, standing a little apart. But it had no flowers. Rhododendrons started flowering only from end of March, through April and early May.

'Good view, but no Kanchenjunga' Roy spoke softly, almost to himself.

Chorten stood a couple of steps behind him, waiting.

'No, no questions.' Roy turned around and smiled. 'I just wanted to find out as to why you became a lama. In all likelihood you joined the monastery at a very early age. Perhaps you were not mature enough to take decisions on your own.'

The young lama remained silent for a while, as if weighing the question.

'Frankly, the decision wasn't mine. It was made by my guardians, particularly by my father, I think. But even if he hadn't wanted to, he didn't have a choice.'

'Why do you say that?'

'Because, the decision had already been taken by my forefathers.'

'Your forefathers? I don't understand.'

Chorten permitted himself a smile. 'It's all preordained. You see, I come from a Lepcha family. And amongst Lepchas there is a long-standing custom—well, it isn't a rule, really, but we abide by it scrupulously, nevertheless. If there are three male progenies born in a household, the second son has to be given away to the monastery, to become a monk.'

'And you happen to be the second son in the family?'

Chorten nodded.

'How quaint! If you were to be the firstborn, or the third or fourth, you wouldn't have been sent?'

'No.'

'Conversely, if your parents had only two sons and, say five daughters, none of them would have been sent?'

'That's right. Now don't laugh.' The young lama seemed to sense some sort of indulgence in him. 'Considering the high rate of infant and child mortality prevailing at that time, the practice made sense, I think.'

'Have you ever regretted being a monk?'

'No. Nor the fact that I am the second male child in the family.' The young lama seemed to weigh his words before saying them. 'On the contrary, I think I am very fortunate to have been chosen to be a monk.'

'Fortunate?' Roy sounded sceptical. 'Obviously, you now

know the price that you have to pay for being a monk? That you have to remain a celibate all your life?'

'What's wrong with celibacy?' Chorten smiled. 'You seem to put a big premium on physical relationships. We don't.'

'But have you never ever contemplated leaving the monastery?'

Chorten tried to remember.

'Yes, perhaps once. But that was a long time ago. We novices were a boisterous, often unmanageable, lot. I think one of us did something pretty naughty and...' Abruptly, Chorten stopped.

'And...' Roy gently pressed him to carry on. 'Perhaps it was an unhappy memory that you don't wish to recall.'

But the young lama had clammed up, simply refusing to be drawn into any further discussion on this.

'Was it severe? Something that left a permanent scar on your mind?'

Just then, one of the young lamas came for Chorten.

'Lama Phunsok has asked for you.'

'Talk to you later.'

Roy watched as Chorten left with the other lama. Come to think of it, the morning hadn't started off too badly. Before coming to Chorten, he had met with two of the seniormost lamas in the monastery, Lama Tshering and Lama Namgyal. While Namgyal had talked to him reasonably freely, Lama Tshering had been much more guarded, sounding hostile at times.

Roy couldn't blame him. Tshering must have guessed something was amiss there that had forced Roy to stay back. No wonder he had resented having conversations with the latter. But it could also be something else. Had there ever been any bad blood between Lama Phunsok and Lama Tshering? A race for the coveted post of the Head Lama, perhaps? And Lama Tshering had lost out? In which case, there could be an undercurrent of resentment and hostility between the two of them, though it was hardly ever likely to come out in the open.

So, could Tshering be the missing link, then? The lama who had aided the theft from inside?

Roy stroked his chin thoughtfully. But there was a question mark against Tenzing as well. The session with him hadn't gone off too well either. Something told Roy that the young lama was hiding something from him, he didn't know what.

What compounded the problem for Roy was the fact that, forget interrogating his suspects, he couldn't even question them about anything openly. It would be tantamount to admitting that the priceless manuscript was missing.

'Miriam...Miriam!' the knock on the door was persistent. 'Are you ready?'

'Ready for what?' Miriam said in a muffled voice, still drying her hair with a towel. She opened the door one tiny bit so she could put one eye through the chink and see who the caller was.

It was one of the maids who worked there.

'Get ready quickly!' There was urgency in the voice. 'Mother Superior wants to see you now.'

But why should Mother want to see her so urgently? An unknown fear gripped Miriam. It was unusual of Mother to call her for anything so early in the morning.

Miriam closed the door and got dressed as quickly as possible. She ran almost all the way to Mother's quarters. There she learnt that Mother was waiting for her in the room adjoining to the prayer hall. When she finally reached the prayer hall she was literally panting. The door to the anteroom was closed. She took a couple of deep breaths before mustering enough courage to knock on the door. At any cost she wanted to regain her composure.

'Yes, come in.' It was Mother's voice all right. She took a moment's pause, tidied up her hair and went in.

'You asked for me, Mother?'

As she stepped in, the first thing that she noticed was the presence of a stranger by Mother's side. It was a middle-aged man of Caucasian origin, wearing an exquisitely cut, dark grey mohair suit. He had pale blue, washed out eyes. Obviously he couldn't be from the church. And yet, Mother treated him so deferentially, as if he was a high church official. So, who was he? Why was he there? And why did he specifically want to meet her, when there were so many others in school? She could feel her heart pounding.

'Don't be so afraid, my child.' Mother superior smiled benignly at her. 'There's nothing to be scared of. Come...'

Miriam slowly went up to Mother and stood with downcast eyes.

'Have I done anything wrong, Mother?'

'No, my dear child, you haven't.' She patted her on the head. 'As a matter of fact, you've been a wonderful girl in our midst, so transparently honest and pure at heart.'

She stood silently, her head bent. A pair of expensive black leather shoes peeped out of the dark trousers. Miriam's covert gaze took in the well-manicured hands, joined at the knees. And on one of the fingers shone a ring the like of which she had never seen before. A red silk kerchief peeped out of the breast pocket of the jacket. The room was filled with an indefinable fragrance which she put down to some perfume or after-shave lotion that the stranger must've been wearing.

Mother Superior stood up and embraced her lightly. 'I shall now leave you to this gentleman. God be with you.'

So saying, she left the room, closing the door behind her. Miriam stood silently, absolutely petrified.

'Your name is Miriam, isn't it?'

She meekly nodded her head. The stranger looked thoughtfully at her, as if her name might signify great portents.

'You've been coming here for how many years now?'

'Five.' She felt so sick that she thought she would swoon any moment now and collapse on the floor in a heap.

'You've been a good Christian…I'm told.'

This required no answer from her. So, she kept quiet.

'Miriam, look at me.'

She felt his eyes piercing through her whole being.

'You needn't be afraid. Look at me.'

She felt an invisible power forcing her to look up at him. The pale blue eyes were unfathomable. She had no idea at all, as to what the brain was thinking behind those eyes.

'As a good Christian you've been specially chosen for a mission. Do not be dismayed. It is not difficult to execute. In a few days you are going to teach, up in the hills, isn't it?'

Her nod was almost imperceptible.

'Good.' At last a thin smile appeared on the stranger's face. 'Now here's what you have to do. But, before that you have to make a promise. Come closer. You will not divulge the contents of this discussion to anybody else, even at the risk of death.'

The stranger's eyes literally bore into her. 'Is that understood?'

It rained unseasonably in the afternoon—a sudden shower that came without any warning. High winds moaned through the closed glass panes of windows. People ran indoors. A solitary crow sat miserably atop a telegraph pole. Blue streaks of lightning zigzagged through dark clouds, freezing the raindrops mid-air. Then came the hailstorm. In no time at all, the courtyard turned snow white. The temperature came down drastically. Gusts of wind made the prayer flags flap loudly in protest.

Only the little lamas of Dengziang seemed to be having the time of their lives, darting in and out of dormitories, gathering hailstones in their maroon gowns and sucking on them, till their tongues became numb with cold and their teeth chattered uncontrollably.

Standing at the corridor of the dormitory, Tenzing surveyed the sky anxiously. As a novice, he was still allowed to go home once a week. That day happened to be today. If the rains didn't stop soon enough he would have to abandon all thoughts of going out. That would make him feel absolutely miserable.

But the rain gods must have been on his side that afternoon. It stopped raining as abruptly as it had begun. He quickly went back inside the dormitory, slung his cloth bag around his shoulder and stepped out. The sky had magically cleared. The lone crow on the telegraph pole was vigorously fanning its wings, sending a fine spray of water particles around. The prayer flags, having shed the raindrops, were merrily fluttering in the air like birds in full flight.

He was feeling quite light-headed as he raced home that afternoon. It was his nephew's birthday. And he had saved up money to buy a chocolate for the little one.

The fact that his brother Johnny was happily married and had begotten children didn't make Tenzing envious at all. He didn't mind the fact that Johnny might be making love to Lara, his lovely curvaceous sister-in-law, every night. No. He didn't spend sleepless nights brooding over that. Work at home and school, and the labours of childbearing would soon rob her of her youth. Already her breasts were beginning to sag. And worry wrinkles had started appearing around Johnny's eyes. Soon enough, he would start returning home late and spend more and more time at the local bar. So, what joys of sex did people talk about? He knew exactly what had transpired between his mom and dad. True, one might say that at the age of fifteen it was too early to talk about a life of celibacy. So he would rather worry about it when the time came.

As he reached the road leading to his home, he could make out even from a distance that their modest home had been given a festive look. Tiny lights twinkled outside. And, inside, the ceilings were decorated with gay festoons. Colourful balloons floated about the room. Tenzing smiled to himself as he noticed furniture in the sitting room. His sister-in-law had recently got a school job. She must have bought the stuff on hire-purchase.

'Ah! There you are.' Everybody cheered as they saw him. 'We were waiting for you.' Johnny came forward and gave him a hug. His nephew, nicknamed Toto, came charging at him. He loved being tossed up in the air by his uncle. Their mom, gone quite grey now, came shuffling to him. As for his father, he was staring down at the rest of the family from the photo on the wall. Tenzing fished out the chocolate from the bag and gave it to his nephew. Toto wanted to have it right then, but was persuaded to have it later. Everyone gathered around the small dining table where a cake had been laid out. Lara had studied at a convent school in Gangtok and made lovely plum cakes. The cake was ceremoniously cut. Toto was given the first piece amidst much photo clicking by Johnny on his cell phone. Mom had prepared thukpa for dinner.

At eight in the evening Tenzing got up to go.

'What is this? You are not going back tonight?' Johnny said.

He missed his brother more than anybody else in the house.

Toto hopped on to his lap and said, 'Stay.'

Tenzing knew exactly what he had to do to appease his nephew. So he tossed him up in the air a couple of times before standing up and stretching himself.

'Mom, the thukpa was really heavenly!'

'But you are not leaving now?' Mom had tears in her eyes.

Even Lara came up and urged him to stay.

'You're still a novice, and permitted to stay with the family once a week, aren't you?'

Tenzing always suspected her to be the most intelligent one in the family.

He sighed and said, 'I have to go back. Got work to do.'

But when he left home he didn't head back to the monastery. He only went back through the road outside his house, as he knew his family would be watching. As soon as he was out of sight, he turned left and took a different route. He walked for a while, peering at the numbers written on the houses from time to time till he found the one he was looking for. He stopped for a moment to get his breath back. He could feel his heart pounding, and he knew it wasn't from the exertion of the walk. He climbed up a flight of steps that took him to a darkened room. He knocked three times on the door and waited. He could hear footsteps approaching the door. Then, a clicking sound—somebody was unlatching the door from inside. The door opened. A dark figure pulled him inside and closed it. And before he could utter a word of surprise, he was plunged deep inside the woman he had hungered for all these years.

It was night. There was not a soul stirring in Dengziang Monastery. Even the sentry at the gate was wrapped in a thick blanket, and barely awake. But at the guest house a solitary light was on in Room Number 106. Inside, Roy was seated at the table with a cup of black coffee in hand. It happened to be the third cup of the evening, and he knew it wasn't going to help him sleep. In front of him, a large, special screen was on, with a whole lot of channels showing on it. These happened to be CCTV footage from cameras positioned at strategic points of the monastery and were set up just a couple of days ago, using the change of lighting system as a cover. Only two people knew about the existence of these hidden cameras, Lama Phunsok and Roy. And only one of them had access to the footage at the moment—Roy.

His eyes were trained on the screen for any unexplained movements occurring on any of these frames. Suddenly, he sat up alert, listening. He thought he could hear a faint humming sound, possibly an approaching car? He listened hard. He was right. It was clear now, the sound of a car climbing uphill laboriously, approaching them. The car seemed to stop just outside the monastery gates. Doors were opened softly, as if to avoid notice, and then closed even more softly. Sound of muffled voices. Then, the car took off again, its sound gradually receding into silence.

He felt tempted to go outside to the balcony, and take a look. But he didn't have to. Presently, he spotted a person on one of the channels on his screen. The figure was wrapped in a shawl, the face almost invisible. It was the sharp clicking sound of the heels that gave her away. He knew now, it couldn't be anyone else but Miriam. By now he was familiar with the style of her walk. He enlarged the particular frame till the shawl-wrapped face was fully visible. The figure quickly approached the guest house, and the oval face looked shiftily around before moving out of the frame.

It was Miriam. He took a sip from the cup to find that the coffee had gone cold. But, it didn't seem to matter, for he downed it all the same. Now, where on earth had Miriam come from so late at night? Was she alone or with somebody else? While he grappled with these questions in his mind, the answer revealed itself fortuitously, on the screen. He had just stifled a yawn and was about to leave the table when another solitary figure appeared in the first frame. It was easy to make out who it was—the yellow-maroon dress and the broad physical frame of the person—easy giveaways. A faint smile appeared on Roy's face as he prepared to go to bed.

The first time Roy had visited the Rabdantse Ruins was in his youth, when he had just completed his masters. He was seriously into trekking those days and had used it as a starting point for a 50-odd-mile route to Yuksom, the original capital of Sikkim. Buddhism didn't hold much attraction for him at that time, and as a result, he had given the Dengziang Monastery a pass. The trekking route to Yuksom led partly through difficult terrain, but didn't involve scaling of great heights. This suited him well as he suffered from vertigo.

He had chosen the place carefully as a secret meeting point with Pradyot, his assistant from Kolkata police. Tourists descended upon this spot in hordes, armed with digital cameras and cell phones, clicked away in frenzy, posed for selfies and posted them on social media instantly, announcing to the whole world that they had been there, and then departed as quickly as they'd arrived.

It was the perfect place for setting up an anonymous meeting.

Roy arrived on foot. It was only a short walk from the centre of the town. He climbed past Yuksom, the only posh hotel in Pelling, with its fancy cottages that clung to the hills, and its exclusive stone paths, and he were suddenly face to face with the Rabdantse Ruins and its silent memories.

He noticed Pradyot had preceded him to the place, clicking with his camera furiously, playing the part of the tourist to perfection. Roy caught up with him from behind, gazing at the mist-topped mountains.

'Nice view.'

Pradyot gave him a perfunctory look and a cryptic 'yah' and carried on clicking.

'No need to take yourself so seriously,' Roy said in an undertone.

But the fellow paid him only scant attention and carried on taking pictures. Roy turned back to face the Ruins.

There was not a soul around.

'I think it is safe to talk now.'

'Are you sure?' At long last Pradyot acknowledged his boss's presence. He lowered the camera and let it hang from his neck. He was seeing his boss just after three weeks or so, but it seemed like ages. Roy had changed. His face looked leaner and sharper. The midriff bulge was missing from the handsome tweed jacket. The eyes behind the spectacles, normally criss-crossed with red veins, were surprisingly clear. It was his boss all right. But different.

'Hope you didn't have any problem getting leave?'

'No, sir.' He didn't wish to elaborate on the innumerable problems he had to face in obtaining this leave, all the more so because his boss was on vacation.

As they strolled past the ruins of the palace and the chortens, Roy briefly outlined the problems at hand. He talked about the rare manuscript, written in Pali, which purported to be on the unknown chapter of Christ's life in India as a Buddhist monk. He talked about the manuscript's secret passage from Leh to Pelling and the fact that someone had stolen it and put Lama Phunsok into great trouble.

'What about the suspects?' Pradyot asked at length.

'Ah! There are some foreign residents at the monastery. All of them could be suspects. Because the Issah manuscript could fetch an astronomical figure in the international market. These foreigners keep going out for sightseeing, to the town, to the neighbouring villages.'

'Why are they here?'

'Most of them are benefactors...donating money to the organization. Some come here to teach.'

'Teach whom?'

'The young lamas, of course! You'll be surprised,' Roy smiled wryly. 'These days junior or trainee lamas are being taught English, Maths and History like in any other school. Even the lamas have to keep up with the times. Why, anything bothering you?'

'Yes,' Pradyot slowly nodded his head. 'This benefactor thing I find rather disturbing. Theoretically, if you donate a very large sum of money, especially in foreign exchange, you could actually influence their decision-making process. Who knows...in lieu of a huge cash donation they might even part with a so-called precious document.'

'You could be right there.'

'So, how many foreigners are there, and what exactly are they doing here?'

'This is why I asked you to come,' Roy smiled in response. 'To keep a tab on them, find out who is up to what.'

He took out his cell phone and started scanning through the pictures.

'Here, take a look.' He zeroed in on a few selected photographs. He had taken them covertly, when no one was watching. One by one he showed Pradyot photos of Billy, Pierre and the silent couple, with short pauses after each one of them. He was about to show him the picture of Miriam when his assistant quipped, 'I believe we have some visitors.'

Indeed, another busload of tourists had just arrived, some twenty of them in all. And shepherding them through the ruins with practised ease was a Lepcha tourist guide who wore a straw hat at a rakish angle. He started to rattle out his spiel in a phony American accent, which was surprising. There weren't too many Americans in this group.

'Take a look, ladies and gentlemen,' he flung out his arms about dramatically, as if he was performing on stage, 'the Rabdantse Ruins represents one of the most important historical landmarks in Sikkim. It was originally built by Tensung Namgyal who shifted capital from Yuksom to this place in the seventeenth century. As for the original palace in Yuksom, nothing remains today.'

He moved past them and the rest of the group followed him. Last amongst them was a young couple, newly married by the look of it. The woman had rather full, red lips, an overtly made-up face and intricate mehendi work all over her arms.

'Now you must be wondering what happened to the royal palace here', carried on the guide. 'Why it is in such shambles today? Puchho puchho?'

Someone in the group asked, 'Why?'

'That's because the Chogyals or kings of Sikkim were devout Buddhists. And in 1814, a terrible thing happened. The Gurkhas invaded Sikkim. As you can imagine the peace-loving Sikkimese were no match for the warlike Gurkhas, who destroyed everything in sight, reducing the palace and the chortens into rubbles.'

In the meantime, the newly married couple had drifted apart from the rest of the group. Slowly, hand in hand, the man and woman walked past him.

'Why does he talk so much, you think?' the woman pointed at the guide.

'That's because he's a guide. And guides earn their living by talking.'

The woman stopped in her tracks and looked around.

'I like this place. What happens, darling, if we stay back here?'

'We miss the bus.'

'Then let's stay back, please.' The woman leaned against the man. 'I find the rest of the group so boring.'

'And then do what?'

By now Roy was hooked on to their conversation.

'Let's see now,' the woman hugged his arms and bit her lower lip provocatively, 'the place gets deserted…and then, we find ourselves a secluded corner and then…you could make love to me. I've always wanted to be made love to under the open sky.'

'Are you serious?' the man looked around him furtively. The girl clung close and inadvertently touched him.

'Oh my god!' she looked down at his trousers in excitement. 'Let's find a place, now.'

Roy walked away from the couple just as the girl turned around to notice him.

'Do you think that taklu overheard our conversation?' giggled the girl.

Roy's hand instinctively reached for the bald patch on his crown. It hurt him to be talked about like that.

'Let him,' the man laughed. 'Who the hell cares?'

And then the couple went out of earshot.

In a few minutes the Rabdantse Ruins was deserted again. The last batch of tourists had boarded the bus and left with the same alacrity that they had arrived with. Roy could not locate the young lovers anymore. Probably they had changed their minds and rejoined the group. Or, better still, found a secluded corner to make love under the open sky.

'Anything the matter?' Pradyot looked enquiringly at his boss.

'No, nothing,' Roy said, eyeing the distant hills. 'There was this young couple in the group. I just happened to overhear snatches of their conversation.'

'Oh! Those two? They stole away through that narrow passage. Out there.'

Pradyot pointed at where the boundary wall had been breached.

They sat down under the shadow of one of the chortens and Roy picked out the next picture on his cell phone for Pradyot to see.

'I've saved her till the end because she's the most interesting of them all. Her name's Miriam.'

'Could you enlarge the face a little?'

Roy did so.

'She seems to be quite a looker, in spite of her baggy outfit.'

'She is preparing to be a nun,' Roy shrugged his shoulders. 'Such a pity!'

Pradyot stole a glance at his boss just to make out if she meant anything to him.

'Don't be ridiculous!' Roy protested, colouring a little. 'Can't one even observe a good-looking woman?'

Though in ruins, the chortens had some broken inscriptions

on them. Roy went up to have a closer look. As he walked around, he kept talking about Miriam.

'She's been coming here for the last five years. Each time, she stays here one to one and a half months at a stretch. Says, she loves teaching the little lamas. 'Could actually be drawn to one of them.'

'But they're only small kids!'

'Yes. It's just that one of them has physically become a man.'

'I see,' Pradyot put a finger on his lips, thinking. Unknowingly, he had started picking up the mannerisms of his boss.

'Could she be interested in the Issah manuscript?'

Roy looked at his assistant. 'Why do you think so?'

'Just thinking aloud. See…she's from the church. And as you yourself said, the church would like to suppress such a document, if it were to exist, at any cost. She's been coming here for the last five years. And she most probably has inside help.'

'Yes, good thinking,' Roy agreed. Just as he was about to change the image, Pradyot interrupted him.

'Can we hold on to her a little longer?' Pradyot peered at the photograph and thought hard. 'I think I have seen her somewhere…somewhere fairly recently.'

Roy smiled indulgently. 'That, I think, is rather unlikely. Unless, of course, you saw her yesterday when you came to see me at the monastery.'

'No, not then…somewhere else.' Suddenly his face brightened. 'Yes. She walked past me this morning on the road.'

'Are you sure? Which way was she headed? Towards the township?'

'No,' Pradyot shook his head. 'I think she was headed towards our hotel. Because beyond our hotel there is nothing else for miles.'

'Sure you aren't making a mistake?'

'I'm sure. She was wearing a very different kind of outfit then, slacks and a tight-fitting jacket. And her face looked unusually pale under the dark parka.'

'Can't, for the life of me, figure out what she could be doing there in the morning,' Roy said, frowning. He remained silent for a while.

'Could it be that she was coming to our hotel to meet someone secretly?'

'That sounds very unlikely,' Roy said, frowning. 'Anyway, about the residents now…Lama Phunsok's own people.' Roy went through some more pictures on the cell phone.

'Now who would've imagined that in the serene, sequestered atmosphere of a Buddhist monastery there could actually be undercurrents of jealousy, competition, even back-stabbing?' Pradyot shook his head in disbelief.

'But true, nevertheless. As Lama Phunsok himself admitted.'

'Who's this?' Pradyot pointed at the picture on Roy's cell phone.

'Lama Tshering, almost as senior as Phunsok. They have a history of bitter rivalry between them, before Lama Phunsok was finally elected the chief of Dengziang.'

'And then?'

'He seems to have accepted defeat in good grace. But, deep inside…you never know. I'm sure he would be delighted if Phunsok gets discredited for the loss of the Issah manuscript.'

'But sir,' Pradyot looked questioningly at his boss. 'Wouldn't he need an accomplice to execute his plan, perhaps, a junior lama?'

Roy smiled in response. 'And this could be the one who's assisting him.' A new picture came through on his cell phone.

'Lama Tenzing.'

Pradyot looked at the picture intently. 'Quite a hulk, isn't he? What would be his height like, 5'10"?'

'Yes. And growing by the day. He isn't sixteen yet, but physically he is a fully grown man.'

'His features are different too. A wide, flat face, broad features.'

'It would mean he is of Tibetan origin. At Dengziang Monastery they prefer to have monks of Tibetan extract.'

'I see,' Pradyot reflected. Then a thought struck him.

'He isn't by any chance the monk close to Miriam is he?'

Roy nodded. 'Lama Tshering and Namgyal, these are the two senior lamas, next to Phunsok. Then there are several junior monks, among them, Tenzing and Chorten.' Roy flashed a new picture on his cell phone.

'Here he is, Lama Chorten, a mild-mannered young monk particularly close to Phunsok. I especially mention these four because, other than Lama Phunsok, usually they are the ones allowed to enter the underground vault.'

'And it is from this underground vault that the Issah manuscript is missing?'

'Exactly.'

In winter the sun sets quite rapidly. Though it was only four in the afternoon, the sky was turning from yellow to red, to crimson, to mauve in quick succession. Pradyot took a look at the sky and unscrewed the camera lens cap to take some pictures with a zoom lens.

In the next few minutes, Roy and Pradyot sat down together to work out the nitty-gritty details of tailing the guests at Dengziang monastery. It was decided that, at least for the time being, the two of them would remain strangers to the outside world. It would allow Pradyot to keep an eye on others, without being observed. Especially if anyone was tailing Roy.

It was the wee hours of the morning when there was a gentle knock on the door. Though Pradyot was sleeping soundly, he was wide awake at the very first knock. At the second knock his hand automatically reached for the small revolver tucked under the pillow and at the third knock he was standing by the door.

'Who is it?' the half-cocked gun was carefully concealed behind him in his right hand.

'I'm Jackie, sir...the hotel boy.'

The door didn't have a magic eye.

'Yes Jackie, what do you want?'

'I came to wake you up sir. To tell you that we are likely to have a super sunrise this morning, at...'

Jackie never had a chance to complete his sentence. The door was suddenly yanked open from inside and before he knew it he was staring into the dark barrel of a snub-nosed revolver.

'Yes Jackie,' Pradyot held the nose of the gun to the man's forehead. 'Did you have to wake me up at this unearthly hour just to inform me about a sunrise on the Kanchenjunga?'

Words had failed Jackie by now. He felt he was dying, choking to death. The cold barrel of the gun, pressed against his forehead, made it impossible for him to breathe.

'Is that why you came to wake me up?' Pradyot whispered into Jackie's ear.

There was a small nod from the hotel boy.

'Well Jackie...don't do it in future. If I want to see a sunrise, you or your reception desk will be duly informed about it. Because...'

Jackie's eyes closed involuntarily as the barrel came to rest between his eyes.

'There wouldn't be a second time. Is that understood?'

Again that infinitesimally small nod from the hotel boy.

'You're free to go now.'

As Jackie attempted to run down the corridor of the second floor, his knees caved in. He fell down on the floor, got up and ran almost like a kangaroo till he was out of sight. Tears streamed down his cheek, tears of relief and joy. At the same time he had the unpleasant sensation of finding his trousers wet.

Normally Pradyot prided himself on the ability to fall asleep at will, anytime, anywhere. But this morning, try as hard as he might, he just couldn't get back to sleep anymore. After struggling till 4.30 a.m., he gave up, got up from the bed, took a shower, then rubbed himself vigorously with a bath towel till blood was pulsing through his limbs. He then made himself a cup of strong black coffee, got dressed, and put the binoculars and the camera inside the bag. The snub-nosed revolver was tucked inside the band of his trousers. Now, coffee mug in hand, he stepped out of the room to the balcony. Pradyot had already figured out that for spying purposes the balcony provided a much better view of the monastery than what he could get from his window. Having balanced the coffee mug on the railing, he brought out a Tupperware container from the outer compartment of his bag. It was supposed to be his ration for on-field duties and contained an assortment of dry fruits. He didn't wish to risk having breakfast either in his room, or at the hotel's dining place for fear of missing out on anything that might be happening at Dengziang.

He took the binocs out and observed the monastery through them, in case something happened there. He watched Pierre's men leave the hotel and pile into vans that would take them to the monastery. It was only a short distance from the hotel, but the steep, winding road made it necessary for them to take a car. The sentry at the gate had gotten used to the crew by now and readily allowed them in. Presently he found Lama Chornum step out of the monk's living quarters and cross over to the main monastery. A young lama walked side by side, someone he couldn't readily recognize. Pradyot had already stored Roy's pictures in his own cell phone and checked them just to make sure.

A little later Lama Phunsok came out of his house in the company of two junior lamas. He could clearly make out who they were—Tenzing and Chorten. He noticed that Phunsok carried a walking stick with him and had considerable difficulty in climbing up the stairs. He idly wondered why they had such steep staircases in all monasteries. The monks weren't particularly tall. Nor were the local people.

Suddenly, Pradyot was wide alert. Two people had come out of the guest house—a man and a woman. This had to be Roy's 'silent' couple. The woman was wrapped in a black shawl and had a pensive look. The man accompanying her had dishevelled hair and hadn't shaved in the last few days.

Quickly Pradyot slung the camera bag around his shoulders and charged down the wide, gloomy staircase to be out of the hotel in a flash. He was half walking, half sprinting now. Roy had told him that the couple vanished for long hours from the monastery and their destination had been a mystery so far. He needed to follow them and find out exactly where they went and why.

Just as he had reached the entrance of the monastery, he saw a blue Omni flash by. He had a fleeting glance of the 'silent' couple, seated inside. Before the car could take a turn and go out of sight, he had a clear view of its number plate. He jotted it down on a small notepad that he always carried with him. Anyway, he wasn't too worried about finding the car later. There couldn't be too many blue Omnis in Pelling with the right tail light missing. He quickly turned around in search of a cab. There were two of them parked outside. But none of them were free to take him as they were carrying passengers.

So, how did the couple manage to get the car? Obviously they had made prior arrangements with the driver. During his visit to the town, Pradyot had noticed a taxi stand near the main market.

Now there was no rush. He walked leisurely back to the hotel, had a hearty complimentary breakfast and ordered reception to arrange for a cab to take him to the town. The first thing he did was to direct the cab to take him to the office of the local taxi association to enquire about the blue Omni.

'Why…have you left anything behind in the cab?'

The secretary of the association was a Nepali guy wearing a black Gurkha cap, with the twin kukri symbol on it.

'No no, it isn't like that,' Pradyot was at his affable best. 'It's just that I find the driver very helpful and amusing.'

The chap at the desk smiled, displaying a silver tooth.

'All our drivers are friendly.'

Pradyot nodded his head in agreement.

'I forget the guy's name though.'

'Toni, sir.'

'Why do all these youngsters have foreign names?'

'Simple, sir,' the man said, grinning. 'That way it's easier for you to remember.'

'This Toni, does he have a phone number?'

The man got up from his desk and called out to one of the cab drivers loitering outside. When the driver came in, he talked to him rapidly in the local lingo and wrote down Toni's phone number on a slip of paper.

'Here…take it.'

Pradyot put the paper in his pocket, thanked the man profusely and gave him five tenners for his efforts.

The man, obviously touched by this unexpected act of

generosity, stood up and shook Pradyot's hand repeatedly. He then produced an old, soiled card from the drawer and handed it over to him. It read—'Praful Rana, Secretary, Pelling Taxi Association.'

'For anything at all, you come to me. I arrange for you.'

Pradyot was already falling in love with the man's silver-tooth smile.

That afternoon the monastery was thrown into quite a flap because of a particular incident. It began with the entry of a nondescript cab entering through its gates, carrying a lone passenger. The person concerned took out a bag from the rear seat of the car, paid the driver and enquired about one Miss Miriam de Gonzales at the reception desk.

There's nothing exceptional about that, except for the fact that this particular visitor happened to be a blue-blooded Christian nun.

Over its colourful long history, Dengziang has had the occasion to receive a stream of the most diverse kind of visitors—political and social dignitaries, state officials, bureaucrats, VIPs, heads of state, even the great Dalai Lama himself. But nobody in his living memory could ever remember having received a Christian nun before. And that too, with a request for overnight stay.

But that was to come later.

The lama at the reception desk was so discomfited by the sudden appearance of this apparition in front of him that, in his hurry to get up from his seat, he sent half the contents of his table flying across the room, littering the floor with papers, files, clips, pencils and markers. This made him even more nervous, as a result of which he froze mid-air, neither being able to sit down nor stand up properly. As a matter of fact, it was the nun herself who had the presence of mind to gather all the loose sheets, files and pens, and the pen stand from the floor and put them back in order on the table.

'I'm so sorry for this sudden intrusion,' she said apologetically, trying her level best to put the embarrassed, blushing lama at ease.

The woman wore black. A black cassock that came down to her heels, covering her legs entirely. A large cross hung from her neck, suspended on a silver chain. She wore thick-framed glasses that covered half of her sallow face. Her thick, matted hair was hidden under a frosty, white cap, the kind usually worn by nuns.

At that time it didn't occur to anyone, but later, it did. In all the five years that Miriam had been coming to the monastery to teach, this was the first time that she had a visitor.

'So…you're here already?' Miriam hastened down the steps when she heard of her friend's arrival. 'I thought you would be coming later.' There was a note of anxiety in her voice.

'Oh! I changed my mind,' the nun said cheerfully. 'Don't tell me you aren't happy to see me.'

'Of course I am! 'Hope the journey wasn't too tiring.'

The women embraced each other, talking animatedly about whatever women talk about when they meet after a long absence. Miriam was shocked to hear that her friend had come all the way from Coorg by train.

'I don't believe this. How many trains did you take in all, then?'

'Stop fussing over me. I'm used to this. You're behaving like a nanny now.'

Hand in hand the two women repaired to Miriam's room. After freshening up, the nun appeared on the first floor balcony to enjoy the afternoon sun.

'The weather's so good here. But it was raining in Coorg when I left.'

Coffee and sandwiches were ordered by Miriam.

Downstairs the lamas spoke in hushed tones, still recovering from the aftershock of their encounter with the nun.

Upstairs too, there was no lack of drama. While the two ladies were engrossed in conversation, Pierre suddenly barged out of his room, attired in nothing but a bathrobe. Water was dripping from his long, curly hair which he shook from time to time, creating a halo effect around his head. His ears were still covered with soapsuds, which would suggest that he had come out in a state of 'bathus interruptus'. Totally oblivious to the presence of the ladies, he paced about the corridor, speaking one moment in a high-pitched voice like a soprano, then bringing down the level to a dramatic whisper the very next.

'*Ah non*, Martin! It's not like that. Everything's proceeding as per schedule.' At this point he got interrupted by whoever the caller was. 'But I…I…' he gasped like a fish out of water. In the next few minutes he tried constantly to interject, but not with much success. He listened for a while and then suddenly butted in with an aggressive 'What do you think?'

By now it was clear that Pierre's patience was wearing out. He burst out with a dramatic swish of his left arm, 'In which case you should have handled it right from the beginning. Yes, damned right!'

He listened some more at this point. Followed by a quickfire, 'Who's preventing you? Ha ha ha!' He burst out laughing, sarcastically.

'You take me for your menial? Then you can shove it up yours for all I care.'

Suddenly, he stopped dead in front of the ladies, cupped his cell phone with the palm of one hand and said, 'What have we got here now...a proper nun! Why are you sermonizing to this pretty lady, may I know? Are you trying to brainwash her to become like you? Not a chance. That will be a public crime, and you know that.'

The two women were left in a state of total shock. Miriam, having been in the guest house long enough, was perhaps aware of Pierre's occasional aberrations. But, this was far worse. He was being positively uncouth. She apologized profusely to her friend for the man's rude behavior.

Strangely though, the nun didn't react at all. Except for a moment of initial irritation, she remained impassive, totally in control. Her cold blue eyes, though, never left his face. Looking at her, Miriam was filled with a deep sense of unease and foreboding, that something catastrophic was likely to befall very soon.

Meanwhile, Pierre ranted in a loud, stagy voice, 'Get thee to a nunnery...to a nunnery!' letting everyone know that he knew his Shakespeare. Having said that, he went back to his room as abruptly as he had come out of it.

'Billy' William Ford had a whale of a time, watching the whole charade from the other end of the verandah. He had come out of his room ostensibly to laze around in the sun and fiddle with his fancy cell phone. He had taken out a chair from his room and had sat down, swinging his feet up on the railing. He didn't really approve of Pierre's conduct, behaving like that in public. But, at the same time, he had no wish to interfere either. After all, it was a free show. And who was he to intervene?

So, just for the heck of it, he shot the whole drama on his cell phone. But how was he to know that what he had shot out of idle curiosity would assume tremendous importance later on?

The blue Omni sped past the market and the cluster of curio shops, past the most well-known orchid house in town and the pork-momo shacks, with their rickety tables and rickety benches, some of them actually mounted on bricks. Gradually, the houses started thinning out. An old wrinkled woman, bent under the enormous weight of the potato sack on her back, carried on in slow motion. As the cloud of dust hit her, she stopped, roundly cursing the driver. A street dog chased a rooster which it thought had strayed into its territory. The rooster flew for its life to the rooftop, flapping its wings and crowing raucously in protest. The dog retaliated by raising one hind leg and pissing at the nearest street lamp. A little girl was trying to kick a plastic football and missing it by a mile. A woman, wrapped in a red-and-black-striped shawl, sat staring at nothing.

The driver turned right and took a dusty road that careened steeply downhill. The old, balding tyres screeched loudly in protest as the car negotiated loose rubble underneath, tilting, bumping and sliding precariously. The driver's hands and feet were continuously in motion, now shifting gears, now stepping on the brakes, releasing the clutch, the steering wheel being constantly manipulated to somehow keep the vehicle on the road. A little later, the engine groaned and almost stalled, going uphill on first gear.

Sitting in the front, next to the driver, Pradyot watched everything, poker-faced, without showing the slightest alarm.

'How much longer, Toni?' Pradyot asked.

They had left the town more than half an hour ago.

'Another five minutes.' Momentarily the driver had taken eyes off the road to look at his watch. That split second loss of concentration sent the car sliding to the very edge of the road and it took all the skill of the driver to bring it under control.

Nobody said anything for a while.

'Do you always drive like this?'

Toni didn't answer immediately.

'I mean, the couple you took to the village this morning...did you drive them like this?'

'Not really.' A faint smile appeared on Toni's face. 'After all, they are middle-aged people.'

'So, you were actually trying to scare the shit out of me?' Pradyot looked speculatively at the driver. 'In future don't try it... or you could be in serious...'

Without bothering to complete the sentence, Pradyot suddenly took charge of the wheel and steered it violently to the left. But, before the car could crash into the rocks, he steered the wheel back, so that the car once again righted itself.

Nobody said anything for a while, though Pradyot could feel Toni's eyes boring into him. The rest of the trip went off uneventfully. Finally, the car stopped. Toni got out and stretched himself.

'We are here.'

Pradyot took his bag from the car and came out too.

'Are we friends, then?'

The driver gave him a slow nod and grinned.

'But no more tricks. Is that understood?'

They shook hands. Pradyot paid him the money and casually asked, 'When do you pick them up again?'

'Don't know.' The driver shrugged.

'They always call me when they're ready. Some days they don't call me at all.'

'Meaning...they stay back in the village?'

'I suppose so.'

Pradyot slung the bag over his shoulder and asked, 'Will you wait for me here? Not more than half an hour.'

Toni looked at his watch and yawned elaborately.

'Sorry, lunch time now.'

Pradyot took out a five hundred rupee note and dangled it in front of him.

'Okay,' the driver grinned. 'I'll have lunch later.'

'Is that the village?' Pradyot pointed at the small cluster of hutments in the distance.

Toni lit a cigarette, squinting against the smoke, and nodded.

'Which house?'

The driver narrowed his eyes and thought. Finally, he shook his head, 'Can't remember.'

'Maybe this will help refresh your memory.'

Pradyot took out a hundred rupee note, then another. Toni still shook his head.

'Think harder.' Pradyot fished out another hundred rupee note. This time the driver smiled.

'Fourth house from the left…the one with the green door and windows.'

Pradyot folded the notes and kept them in the driver's shirt pocket before walking away.

There was a brick road that led to the village. Strictly speaking, it was a misnomer to call it a village. There were hardly eight to ten hutments huddled together. The cottage with the green door wasn't hard to find. The owner of this place seemed to be in a somewhat better financial condition than the rest. The house had proper fencing, even if it was in a rickety condition, and a proper wooden gate, painted white. A pebbled path led from the gate to the cottage. On either side of the path there were flowerbeds, displaying petunias, geraniums and gladiolas. Near the cottage stood a squash tree, laden with fruits. But, it seemed nobody ate them, because there were quite a few of them, lying sodden on the ground.

Pradyot opened the coppice gate and entered the house. Immediately, a furry dog came charging in from the back of the house and barked furiously at him. Pradyot stood still. He had no wish to be bitten by a dog in a godforsaken place like this where he wasn't sure tetanus would be readily available. After a few minutes' barking, the main door of the cottage opened just a little and a face peeped out.

'Who you want?' the man looked suspiciously at Pradyot. 'There is no one in house.'

'What about you?'

The man considered the question for a while before answering. 'I just work here. Hey Dodo! Keep quiet.'

The dog kept on barking.

'I want to talk,' Pradyot said.

'I no one.' The man simply shook his head and shut the door behind him.

Pradyot stood there for a while, waiting. But no one emerged from the house. And the dog kept on barking non-stop. Soon enough he realized that barking dogs seldom bite. Boldly he walked up to the door and knocked. Nothing happened. No one came out. So he knocked again. This time he kept on knocking, till someone was forced to open the door. It was the same face.

'I said...'

'Shut up and listen, will you?' Pradyot shouted at him. It was a calculated risk. And it seemed to work. The man looked uncertainly at him.

'The foreign couple...white skin...husband and wife...I know they came here.'

Just for a second fear showed on his face and he stole a glance behind him.

'No no...nobody come here. No foreigner. You go. Or I call up neighbour.'

Pradyot stared hard at him, swearing under his breath before leaving. He came out of the house, closing the gate behind him. The dog kept barking without any let-up. He left the house and kept on walking. The dog finally went inside and the man closed the door. Pradyot stopped, retraced his steps to return to the cottage preceding the one he had been to. He went around it and then doubled back to come and stand at the rear of the house. The exit door was shut. So were the windows. He couldn't look through the window panes as they were curtained.

He stood there, thinking. He could stay back and wait for the couple to emerge from the house. But, there was no surety as to when they would return, or whether they would return that day at all. And, even if the 'silent' couple were to emerge now, what would he do? He couldn't accost or interrogate them, could he? They had simply come to pay a visit to this house. And that couldn't be construed as a crime.

He returned to the car and asked Toni to drive back to the monastery. In a way, his mission had been accomplished; at least partially. He knew now where the couple went in the village, though not why. The why part could be easily found out by informing the local police.

Coffee mug in hand, Roy sat glued to the large screen on the table. He had hardly moved out of his room since his return from Rabdantse yesterday. There were specific instructions that breakfast, lunch and dinner should be sent up to him. There would be a gentle knock on the door. Thereafter, the bearer would leave the food tray outside his room. Just that. Nobody, but nobody, was allowed inside.

There was a reason for all this secrecy. He had converted his room into an espionage centre. Mounted on his table was a large screen that showed, section by section, CCTV footage of every important area of the monastery.

In the morning he had watched the 'silent' couple leave the guest house, exit through the gate and wait outside. A little later he had observed the blue Omni arrive, pick them up and leave in a mushrooming cloud of black smoke. Small cars had only a limited life span in the hilly regions.

And just as the Omni was speeding away, he had noticed Pradyot arrive from the right in a mad rush. He had been tempted to call up his assistant and provide him with the number of the car. But he knew it would not only be unnecessary, but also unwelcome from his assistant's side. He had given the latter the space to grow, instead of looking over his shoulders all the time. And that had worked. In the last three years Pradyot had grown into a 'pro'.

Roy's eyes flitted from frame to frame with hawk-like intensity, keeping a sharp watch on whatever was happening in the monastery.

In the afternoon, there was a gentle knock on the door. He heard the soft shuffle of feet outside his room as the waiter left the lunch tray on the floor. But he felt no inclination to step outside and fetch his food. Endless cups of black coffee had killed his appetite.

And then it happened. A private cab appeared outside the gate. It wasn't the one that had picked up the 'silent' couple in the morning. This car, too, was an Omni, but red in colour. Roy sat upright on his chair as he noticed the passenger step out of the cab. It was a nun of Caucasian origin. A starched white cap covered her hair completely. She wore powerful, thick classes and a black cassock.

He was plainly intrigued. Was she a regular tourist? Why would she, obviously a Catholic nun, visit a Buddhist monastery? Just for the heck of it? Or was there any other reason?

All these questions were soon resolved for him. The red cab, after dropping her, headed back to the town. Tourists visiting Dengziang seldom gave up their cabs, for the town happened to be more than five kilometres away.

So obviously she had come to meet somebody in particular. Was it Miriam? Or could it be Lama Phunsok? It might sound a little far-fetched, but could she possibly have come here as an emissary of the church with a secret proposal...the Issah manuscript in lieu of a huge amount of cash?

Even this question was resolved for Roy soon enough. After talking to the sentry the nun headed straight for the guest house. So Lama Phunsok was out. Miriam was in. Now why did she have to come and meet Miriam all of a sudden? Was it something urgent, an emergency? Did it have anything to do with the Issah manuscript? Or was it something else?

A whole lot of questions swirled through his mind, with no clear-cut answers.

Had things come to a head, then? Were they planning to remove the manuscript that night itself? In which case the manuscript had to be hidden somewhere within the four walls of the monastery. If Miriam was the nun's conduit, which would be a reasonable supposition, she had to have a connection with someone inside. And here the only monk that she could possibly be close to was Tenzing.

In all probability, then, Tenzing was going to collect the document that night from its hidden place and pass it on to Miriam. Miriam, in turn, would hand it over to the nun. The latter, in all likelihood, would make off with the document early next morning.

Roy stifled a yawn with the back of his hand. He knew it was going to be a long night.

The last rays of the sun made the sky bleed. It was as if tufts of cloud were used as cotton buds to stem the flow of blood from some deep invisible wound. Miriam and the nun had been served fresh cups of coffee and snacks, and were obviously enjoying the scenery.

'Such a pity that I didn't bring the camera with me,' said the nun regretfully. 'It would have made such a lovely photograph.'

'In which case you should've come in the morning,' said Miriam. 'You could get such a splendid view of the Kanchenjunga then!'

'Kanchen…?'

'Kanchenjunga,' Miriam pointed towards the western sky. 'The third highest mountain peak in the world.'

'Is it so? How interesting!'

'Maybe tomorrow you should try again.'

'Yes. Maybe.' The nun looked thoughtfully at her.

A gust of cold wind made Miriam shiver a little. She wasn't wearing anything warm.

'Let's go down to our room.' So saying, she got up from the chair.

'Let's, er… Miriam, it shouldn't be too much of a problem if I were to stay with you tonight, would it?'

'You want to stay with me? Well, I really wouldn't know.' Miriam looked doubtfully at her own toes. 'Have to check with the authorities here.'

'Is it so? Let's get it done, then, without any further delay,' the nun responded on a brisk note.

Together they went down to the reception counter. The lama at the desk looked doubtfully at the nun.

'See Miriam…your request is highly unusual. We don't, as a rule, allow outsiders to stay here, you know that.'

Miriam glanced at the nun and smiled back.

'But she isn't an outsider. She's my friend!'

'I know. But all the same.'

The nun intervened at this point.

'Just for one night, please.'

The monk looked back at them without saying a word, but held his ground.

'You see my problem…' the nun looked at the lama guiltily. 'I haven't arranged for any accommodation tonight.'

'Maybe I could talk to Lama Phunsok about it,' Miriam said hopefully.

The monk at the counter looked immensely relieved.

'Yes, that would be best.'

In the last five years Miriam had grown popular not only with the students, but with the rest of the monks as well. Lama Phunsok, in particular, had become extremely fond of her; charmed by her sincerity of purpose, diligence and sweet manners.

'All right…since this is a special request, Miriam,' Phunsok conceded. 'But only for tonight.'

'Only for tonight,' responded the nun gratefully.

That night Roy didn't get even a wink of sleep. Sitting at the table, he guzzled cup after cup of strong black coffee to keep himself awake. His eyes flitted from frame to frame on the large screen, his body taut as a bowstring, waiting for something to happen.

But, to his utter surprise, nothing seemed to happen. No one slipped out of his or her room and darted across the courtyard, or scurried about in the dark recesses of the monastery in search of the elusive manuscript. It was as if everybody had collectively conspired against him to prove him wrong about his hunch that something would happen that night.

But Roy hadn't taken any chances. While he had mounted a continuous vigil on the inmates of the monastery through CCTV, he had enlisted the help of two additional men to keep an eye on the exit point. One was the sentry at the gate. He was told to subject anyone getting out of the monastery that night or the morning next to the most vigorous body search. The second person he had engaged to keep a lookout that night was Pradyot, his assistant.

But where on earth could the manuscript be hidden? Roy racked his brains in search of an answer. Since it wasn't inside the vault, could it have been slipped into the library on the first floor? It was such an obvious place that nobody would ever suspect it to be there. Or was it in somebody's room? If so, it had to be in the room of one of the lamas. Certainly not in the guest house. Could Lama Tshering be hiding it to discredit Lama Phunsok? If he was, he would have made his move by now; to bring to public notice that the Issah manuscript was missing. Or, was it any of the other senior lamas in cahoots with the Rhumtek monastery? He wasn't sure. But at least the nun's presence would suggest the exchange was likely to be made that night itself. How was it going to be passed on to Miriam? Should he barge into her room and order a thorough search? What if all this was a wild goose chase?

Deep into the night the owl hooted twice, followed by the crowing of a rooster, which must have mistaken the moonlit night for dawn. Suddenly he thought he heard the muffled cry of a woman. He rushed out to the balcony and listened. But after that there was nothing. Could he have imagined the woman's cry? Where did it come from? The only woman residing in the guest house was Miriam.

Roy wasn't going to take any chances. He gumshoed down the steps to the ground floor and waited, crouching outside Miriam's room.

But her room was enveloped in darkness. And it was silent. Roy waited with bated breath, his ears glued to the door, for a long time. If only he could hear the tiniest sound emanating from the room, the faintest squeak, garbled voice or a groan, he wouldn't hesitate to act. If necessary, he would wake up everyone in the monastery and forcibly enter the room.

Suddenly an unpleasant thought struck him. Could it be that the two women were engaged in some kind of a physical relationship? Was the woman's cry one of ecstasy? No no, how could that be? What about her relationship with the monk then? Wasn't she supposed to be in love with Tenzing? Or was it all a façade? Only a trap, to get hold of the manuscript?

Roy deliberated for a long time, rooted outside her door. In the end, however, he decided to go back to his room.

It was a brilliant sunlit morning. The entire monastery was awash with a golden light. In the distance the Kanchenjunga was visible in all its splendour. A thick layer of clouds at the bottom of the mountain made the golden peak float mid-air.

The first batch of tourists had started arriving in vans, trekkers and SUVs. The entire monastery was filled with laughter and gaiety. Pierre had arranged for a special shoot of the little boys in their gold and maroon clothes to pass in a single formation on the foreground, while the majestic Kanchenjunga filled the backdrop.

After a night of fruitless vigil, Roy hit the bed. He had already received an update from Pradyot, and made sure no one had left the monastery the night before. His head felt like it weighed a tonne and he could hardly keep his eyes open. Perhaps the tension of last night was also telling on him. But try as hard as he might, he couldn't get any sleep. After half an hour of turning and tossing about, he gave up. He got up from the bed, stripped himself and stood under the cold shower till his teeth chattered. He then dressed and left the room after securely locking the door, and went down to the courtyard.

He desperately needed some fresh air. For a change, Pierre was in a cheerful mood, not foul-mouthing his unit boys. Over the course of the last few days, his shooting had gone rather well. And now he was in the process of winding up. Spotting Roy in the crowd, he beckoned him to come and have a look. They were shooting with a camera which, for some strange reason, they called Red. The camera was black in colour. There was a monitor attached to the camera on which you could see exactly what was being shot.

'In the celluloid days you had to wait for the first prints to be certain of what had been canned.'

'How you are shooting now...it's not on celluloid?'

'Which age are you from, Roy...the Stone Age?'

Pierre had at last got his chance to show off to him.

'So how are you shooting on now?'

'Digital, man! The whole world's gone digital, leaving you behind.'

Roy went closer and looked through the monitor.

Pierre threw a thick black cloth over him, covering up the monitor. 'This way you'll see better.'

The shot was, indeed, spectacular. Pierre had arranged to have the boys cross the camera in a profile formation. As for the boys, they were giggling and laughing with joy, and quite understandably so. They had been spared the daily drudgery of studying religious scriptures and had been given the day off for the shoot. Their ruddy cheeks showed like Kashmiri apples on the monitor.

'Run…my babies, run!'

At Pierre's command the boys started running.

'We are shooting in slow mo now.'

Their maroon chaddars started flying in the wind, as if each one of them had grown wings. It was, indeed, an incredible shot.

'Bravo!' exclaimed Roy and shook hands with Pierre warmly.

'I'm good, man, I'm good,' Pierre said with a smug smile.

Trust Pierre to beat his own drum.

Just then there was a noise from behind. It seemed to come from the direction of the guest house. Roy turned around, frowning. And, then suddenly, every cell in his body was galvanized into action. He ran back as fast as he could. As he raced and turned into the ground floor corridor of the guest house, he skidded to a halt. There were people standing outside Miriam's door, speaking in hushed tones.

After that everything seemed to be happening in slow motion. He was running towards Miriam's room, but his steps seemed to move ever so slowly. As if the air had become so thick, it was impossible to move forward.

There were lamas guarding the door. Someone said, 'She's committed suicide.' Roy pushed him aside and went in. There she was, Miriam, sleeping peacefully on the bed. Roy looked at his watch. It was ten past ten. The time when time stands still.

Pradyot had asked the hotel to pack some dry food for him in a disposable box. And piping hot black coffee in a steel flask. All this was in preparation for, what he liked to call, the night watch. He had then parked himself a little distance from the monastery gate, concealed under the shadows of a tree. The road, in any case, was dimly lit. Knowing that the night ahead would be long and bitterly cold, he had put on a thick, old army jacket with a hood and zipped it up to his neck. Leaning against the tree, he slowly munched cold chicken sandwich, with occasional sips from the flask.

Perhaps it would have been better if he had brought some rum with him. But he didn't wish to take the risk. Who knows, it might just slow down his reflexes, or cloud his judgment.

In many ways Pradyot was a bit of a loner. He was comfortable being with himself. And these kind of long waits allowed him that privacy. He had this happy knack of allowing his body to go in sleep mode, while his mind would remain razor sharp alert.

The night wore on. Nothing happened except for the creepy sensation of a worm crawling down his neck for warmth. He drew away from the tree and sat down on hard ground. The gatekeeper at the monastery was softly humming some Lepcha tune, which the stillness of the night carried to him. After a while he got up from the ground and dusted himself. It was the ants this time.

The night was getting bitterly cold. Hands inside the army jacket, he walked about briskly. The sentry at the gate had stopped humming long back, probably ensconced himself inside a blanket, and was happily asleep now. He downed the rest of the coffee in one gulp. It didn't help much. The coffee had turned lukewarm. He looked up. The sky had taken on a bright indigo sheen in the moonlight. Stars winked on and off.

By 4.30 a.m., the eastern sky behind the monastery began to lighten. At 5.30 a.m., he was witness to the most glorious sunrise ever on the Kanchenjunga. From pink to gold to yellow—the colours on the peak changed by the second. Without knowing why, he sank to his knees in gratefulness.

At 7 a.m., he returned to the hotel and texted Roy. 'No one's come out, sir. I am back in the hotel.' Even after he was back he never left his watch. He carried his black coffee to the second floor portico which provided him with a commanding view of the monastery. At 10 a.m., he went briefly back to his room for a shower. But when he returned to the portico, he sensed something amiss. He saw Roy, who had been chatting with Pierre till then, rush back towards the guest house. He knew that moment that something had gone grievously wrong. Pradyot quickly ran downstairs and soon entered through the gates of the monastery as a tourist.

Roy walked softly, almost on tiptoes, to the bed, as if afraid of waking her up. Miriam seemed to be sleeping peacefully, her hands neatly folded just below her breasts. Routinely his left hand went down, the fingers feeling for the pulse just behind the ear.

Nothing. No movement there. Her chest did not heave. His mind went back to the sunny morning when they had walked down to the town together. How, on their way back, they had this miraculous escape from the jaws of death. How he had held her in his arms, protecting her from the mass of falling debris. The warmth of her body against his. He remembered it all.

Had he actually fallen a little in love with her? Well, if he had, it didn't matter anymore.

He looked at her not as Miriam, but as any other dead body. The hands folded under her breasts…wasn't that a little too neat, too pat? Did she put an end to her own life with an overdoze of sleeping pills?

Possible. He remembered she had once attempted suicide by slashing her own wrist. But that was a long time back. Would she have wanted to take her own life today? Especially when she was possibly having an affair with one of the young lamas there? Doubtful.

So actually it could be murder, made to look like suicide. He searched under the pillow and the bed, just in case she had left any note behind. Nothing there.

His eyes shifted to the table. There were two glasses lying there, one of them half empty. He walked across to the table, dipped a finger into the half-empty glass and put the finger into his mouth. The liquid tasted sweet, probably had cocoa and malt in it. So, in all probability, it was some kind of a health drink. A perfect nightcap before going to sleep.

The question was whether the drink was spiked or not. And,

if it was, only one of the glasses was likely to be spiked, the one from which Miriam had drunk. Taking out a handkerchief from his pocket, he carefully lifted the empty glass from the bottom and held it against the light. There it was, a faint stain on the rim, most likely a lip mark, as he slowly turned it around. He thought he could spy faint fingerprints on the glass as well.

Of course, forensic tests would reveal whose lip mark and fingerprints were on the glass. But he was more or less sure that it would be Miriam's. He brought the glass close and sniffed at it, but couldn't detect any definitive smell.

The half-empty glass was more puzzling. As Roy held it against the light, he found no marks either on the rim or any other part of the glass. It could only mean one thing—the glass had been carefully wiped clean after use. Deliberately. A grim smile appeared on Roy's face. He knew he was dealing with a 'pro' here. He had a sinking feeling that every object that the nun might have touched, or come into contact with, had been methodically wiped clean. Try as they might, neither he nor the police were likely to find any trace of the nun in the room.

He walked back to Miriam, bending over her to take a closer look. If it was murder, maybe he could find some clue somewhere? He inspected her face intently. Her hair was covering part of her throat. Was that natural? There was only one way to find out. Using a ball pen to shift her hair away, he looked again. There were faint violet marks on her throat.

He tried to figure out what might have happened last night. They had a drink together after dinner, a drink most likely prepared by the nun. But, when did she spike Miriam's drink? When the latter had gone to the washroom? Quite likely. After drinking both of them had gone to bed. The nun had waited for Miriam to fall asleep. And then she had choked her to death?

But then, that didn't quite explain the tiny scratch marks and abrasions on her hands. So, was there a scuffle? Possibly. The nun had thought there would be no resistance from Miriam's side. But she had been surprised. Miriam perhaps did wake up as she was being throttled, and put up a fight.

But the clean sheets? The nun had probably tidied them up after the act. But, why did the nun have to murder Miriam? Certainly not out of jealousy? Let's say the nun had come here because she believed the Issah manuscript was already with Miriam. But, Miriam might have said she didn't have it, which the nun didn't quite believe. Therefore, the need to do away with her, so she could conduct a thorough search for the manuscript amongst her possessions.

But, if the nun had put sleeping pills or some kind of soporific in Miriam's drink, why the fight? Why the need to kill her? Perhaps because the drink didn't quite have the desired effect on her. Perhaps she had sensed something wrong in the drink, gone to the bathroom, thrown up the drink and flushed it down the toilet.

Suddenly he felt madly angry, not so much with the nun as with himself. If he had only acted on his instincts last night when he thought he heard the muffled cry of a woman and had come down the steps and stood waiting outside her door! Who knows, if he had only forced his way in at that juncture he might even have been able to save her? And surely he would have been able to apprehend the nun, catch her red-handed?

Instead, he had done nothing, paralyzed by the fear of being made a public fool. And now the girl was dead. How he wished he could have the whole thing played out again! So he could take corrective actions this time. But, in life there are no retakes, as Pierre would have told him. No amount of self-recrimination would bring her back. He felt inconsolably sad. It wasn't right that so beautiful a woman should die so young.

As he sat still, his mind came to a resolve. The least he could do was to avenge her death, catch the nun before she did the vanishing trick. He glanced at his watch. Any moment now the police were likely to come in and take over the case. Before that happened, he needed to go through Miriam's belongings quickly to check if there was anything missing. He located her suitcase lying on the wooden rack, next to the wardrobe. It was closed, but fortunately for him, not locked. At first sight, all her clothes looked all nicely folded and untouched. But, on closer scrutiny, he thought there were signs that they had been hastily rearranged. He went through each of the items in the suitcase, taking care to put them back just as he had found them. Under the lid there was a special compartment. He unzipped it, slipped his hands inside and came up with a few of her things. But as soon as he had taken a look, he dropped them like hot potatoes. They were Miriam's most intimate things—bras and panties, some of them embellished with silken, lacy frills. So, even nuns wore bras and panties underneath their clothes, he thought, bemused. But the very next moment he felt ashamed of himself. A nun, too, was a woman, not a sack of potatoes.

As he took a last look at the contents of the suitcase, nothing seemed to be amiss. But then, if the manuscript had been hidden there, it was obviously gone now.

He turned his attention to the wardrobe. Miriam's clothes were neatly hung from hangers on the top compartment. He shifted them one by one and found nothing. At the bottom compartment there was a large, quilted cotton bag with a nice floral pattern. He unzipped the bag and rummaged through its contents. Here everything was in a topsy-turvy condition, as if a lawn mower had gone through it. So the nun had gone through Miriam's belongings all right.

The big question was, did she find what she was looking for? He was reasonably sanguine that it had to be the Issah manuscript and nothing else.

Roy closed the wardrobe and came to the table, looking around. Was Miriam carrying a personal laptop or a tab by any chance? If she did, it could throw up a lot of vital information. But sadly, no such thing could be found in her room. It might be worthwhile to check with her young pupils, if she had carried one. But then again, it wouldn't help with the case if they said she had one and now it was missing. Roy went across to the washroom and went through the medical cabinet, towel racks, everything. Nothing suspicious anywhere.

He came back to the room and stood over the bed. Just then there was a stir near the door. He looked up to find people making way for Lama Phunsok. He also spotted Pradyot, standing in the background and trying to catch his attention. Roy asked one of the lamas to let him in. Leaning heavily on his walking stick, the elderly lama came and stood by his side.

'I…I simply can't believe this! It's not possible…she can't be dead.' Phunsok's words were punctuated by sharp gasps. He looked so shattered he would've certainly collapsed on the floor if Roy hadn't supported him in the nick of time. A lama fetched a chair and helped him sit down.

'Someone said she's committed suicide. Miriam's such a happy child. Why should she want to do that?'

Roy gently broke the news to him.

'I'm afraid it looks like murder, not suicide.'

Phunsok looked aghast. 'No, this can't be. A girl of such good spirits! And such a sweet disposition! Why should anyone want to murder her?'

Rhetorical question. Roy decided not to answer it.

'You know, she was such a good teacher'. Phunsok simply couldn't stop talking about her. 'So popular with my boys. And such a wonderful human being!'

Roy gently placed his hand on the lama's.

'I know.'

At that moment a comforting hand came and rested on his shoulders. He turned around to find Pradyot standing behind him.

'It's the nun, isn't it?'

Suddenly, for no reason at all, his vision got slightly blurred.

'Who was the first to find her?'

Murders didn't take place too often in Pelling. So Chief Inspector Narsingh Thapa decided to make an exception by personally appearing at Dengziang, instead of relegating the job to one of his assistants.

'Me, sir,' Lama Tashiding answered.

'Would you care to explain how you found her?'

'Sir… I was at the reception this morning when this lady came to me and said she was going out for her morning walk. And…'

'Yes, carry on.'

'She asked me not to wake up Miriam madam too early, saying they had chatted with each other the whole night.'

'Which lady is this?'

'A middle-aged Christian lady… a nun, I think. She stayed with her last night.'

'A nun in the monastery?' Thapa raised his eyebrows theatrically.

'Indian or foreigner?'

'Foreigner, sir.'

'What time was it when she left?'

'7.30-8 a.m., sir.'

'7.30 or 8?' It was clear that Thapa was a stickler for certitudes.'

'Didn't look at the watch, sir.'

Thapa let out an exasperated sigh, then turned to his assistant.

'Tejpal, call up the station right away. Find out if any foreign nun has been seen in Pelling in the last few days. Also, check out with all the hotels and guest houses in town if she had checked in at any one of them. If anyone else finds her, hold her up for questioning.'

Inspector Tejpal was about to leave the room when he was called back.

'And oh...before I forget, call up the secretary of Pelling Private Taxi Association, whatever his name is, and find out which of our taxis have been used by this nun. She must have used a cab to move around in Pelling.'

'Yes, sir.' Tejpal saluted smartly and left the room.

'Maybe...I could be of help.'

Thapa turned around and looked at Roy for the first time.

'And you are...?' he asked, frowning.

'Avinash Roy from Kolkata...been staying here at the monastery for the last three weeks.'

'Three weeks is a long time to spend in a godforsaken place like Pelling. May I know why?' While the question was directed at Roy, Thapa looked askance at Lama Phunsok.

It was somewhat unusual for an Indian to stay at the monastery guest house, and Thapa was well aware of it.

'He received permission to stay here, Inspector,' Phunsok replied frostily. 'Mr Roy is deeply into Buddhism...if you insist on knowing.'

'Oh!' Thapa was about to add 'holy cow', but refrained from saying so. Nevertheless, his hands went up in mock horror.

'I've come here as a tourist,' Roy said simply.

Inspector Thapa seemed not to hear it.

'And how, may I ask, do you propose to help us?'

'The nun came here in a tomato-red Omni yesterday... sometime in the afternoon. Around 2.30 p.m., give and take a few minutes.'

The implied dig about 'time' was not lost on Thapa.

'Oh really! For a lay person you seem to remember an awful lot of things. Maybe you'd remember the licence number of the car as well.'

The admiration in his voice was tinged with sarcasm.

'Sorry, I don't remember that. But that could be ascertained from the taxi stand. There aren't too many tomato-red taxis around in Pelling.'

Roy could have easily gone back to his room and fetched the information, but chose not to. It would've created complications about how he had come to know about it.

'Thanks all the same, Mr Roy, you should've joined the intelligence.'

'Er... I work for Kolkata police,' Roy admitted with modesty.

'Ha ha ha! I should've known.' Thapa raised his left eyebrow theatrically.

'If ever I'm stuck on this case now I know who to approach for help.'

But the manner in which it was said made it clear that such an eventuality would be quite remote.

'Oh, Tejpal!' Inspector Thapa called up his assistant on the cell phone. 'Your task has been made so much easier now, thanks to our detective friend from Kolkata. I'm told that the nun had arrived at the monastery in a tomato-red Omni car. Yes, you heard me right. So, finding the cab driver should be a piece of cake now. Bring him over ASAP.'

Roy smiled to himself. Thapa was out to prove that, though posted in a far-flung territory, he was *au fait* with today's vocabulary.

'Those who are not required here may please leave the room. I shall ask for them as and when required,' Thapa said with bustling efficiency.

Pradyot cast a silent look at Roy and left.

'No no…you two don't need to go.' Thapa indicated that Roy and Phunsok should stay back.

'Now we can get down to business. Lama, Lama…?'

'Tashiding.'

'Sorry to forget your name, Lama Tashiding. The nun left and, by the way, does anybody know her name?'

Tashiding and Phunsok looked at each other and shook their heads. Apparently no one knew her name.

'You…Mr Roy? Since you seem to know everything?' Thapa politely enquired. 'Would you know her name?'

'No, actually I never had the occasion to ask her.'

'I see. So after the nun left you went back to your desk?'

'Yes, sir. That I did. But around 9.30–10 a.m. I got a little worried.'

'Worried…why?'

'You see, Miriam is an early riser. She teaches our young monks English and Maths. And…she's very punctual.'

'You mean used to be.' He said, indicating her dead body. 'Miriam's no more.'

Confronted with the unpleasant reality of Miriam's death, Lama Tashiding was suddenly at a loss for words.

'It was most unusual of her to sleep so long. So I went to her room and rang the doorbell. Then I knocked on the door. But there was no response from her. So I sent a message to him,' Tashiding said, indicating Lama Phunsok, 'and had the door forced open.'

'And then?'

'As I entered the room I initially thought she was sleeping. Then I came close to her and called her by her name loudly. She didn't respond. So I looked intently and noticed she wasn't breathing at all. It was then that I got really scared and called people in.'

'Did you touch her body at any point?'

'No sir. Why should I?'

'Sure you are not covering up?' Thapa looked shrewdly at the young lama. 'Maybe just out of curiosity…you touched her to find out if her body was still warm or not.'

'No, I didn't.' Tashiding looked helplessly at Lama Phunsok.

'We are not used to people lying,' Lama Phunsok quickly sprang to the young lama's defence.

The Chief Inspector didn't say anything in response. But the smile on his face clearly indicated that he didn't give too much credence to the senior lama's assertions.

'By the way, the nun had said she was going out for a morning walk. Did she return at all?'

'No.'

'It didn't strike you as something unusual?'

Tashiding remained sullenly silent.

'Anything else comes to your mind?'

Tashiding simply shook his head.

Clearly Thapa had lost a sound and cooperative witness. Maybe he had become aware of it, for he glanced uncomfortably at Roy.

'All right Lama Tashiding, we're through with you for the time being,' Thapa said dismissively. 'But, should the need arise, you'll be available for further questioning.'

The last few words were more directed towards Lama Phunsok than Tashiding.

Roy was privately amused, but kept a stony face.

'Er... Lama Phunsok, what is your opinion of the deceased?'

'As a human being? She was very charming and a warm, decent human being. Very popular with the boys.'

'I see... and what about the seniors?'

'She was equally popular with the senior lamas, if that's what you want to know.'

'Her being a Christian, and close to the missionary, didn't pose any problems for you at any stage?'

'Should it?' Lama Phunsok responded with a ready smile. 'Buddhism never was, nor is, against plurality of faith.'

'Hmm...' Thapa seemed to carefully ponder over these words. 'How well do you know her?'

'She's been coming here... sorry, was coming here, for the last five years. We have her residential address. It's near Coorg. We also have the address of the missionary school where she used to teach. And I believe she was living there for the last two years.'

'At the missionary school? It would be a big help if we could have both the addresses then.'

Phunsok immediately ordered one of the lamas to fetch Miriam's address from the register book at the office.

'Anything else?' Phunsok looked sharply at Thapa.

'Yes. I'm particularly curious about her private life. Did she have any friends here, anyone special?'

Phunsok considered the question for a while.

'You mean boyfriend?'

'Yes... the usual relationship between a man and a woman.'

'No,' Phunsok shook his head. 'I can't think of anyone.'

'Are you aware of the fact that Miriam's might not be a case of suicide, but murder?'

'Yes, that's more or less what I have been told by Mr Roy.'

Thapa cast a suspicious glance at Roy, but didn't pass any comment.

'Now, if it's murder, she must have made some enemies. Would you know of any?'

Lama Phunsok shook his head.

'Anyone that you might suspect?'

'I can't. I can't think of anyone vile enough to want to murder her.'

'What do you know about the nun and her relationship with Miriam?'

'Very little. Just that I met her for the first time yesterday evening. Miriam came to me with her, requesting if her friend could stay with her for one night.'

'And you granted her permission?'

'We do not, as a rule, allow outsiders to stay at our guest house. But, in Miriam's case, we made an exception.'

'So you admit what you did was irregular so far as the nun was concerned?'

Phunsok nodded his head. 'And I bitterly regret the decision.'

'So, you also admit that the nun was the cause of Miriam's death?'

'That's what it looks like, doesn't it? Or do you suspect somebody else?'

Thapa gave a thin smile in answer.

'I thought I was supposed to do the questioning.'

'It's not for me to tell you what you should be doing, but I think your first priority is to trace the nun and arrest her.'

Thapa nodded grimly. 'The police are already looking for her in Pelling. Maybe it's a good idea to send a statewide alert for the nun.'

Thapa called up the station and spoke with someone on the matter.

'Does anyone have a photograph of this woman?'

Thapa looked around. But nobody said yes.

'Mr Roy? I don't expect the lamas to be so inquisitive. But you would be the person most likely to have taken her photograph.'

'Unfortunately, I never had the chance to meet her personally.' Roy answered politely. 'In any case, I'm not in the habit of taking pictures of nuns.'

'Ha ha ha! I quite like your dry sense of humour. But I hope you are not averse to answering a few questions on Miriam.'

'Anything I can do to catch the culprit.'

'This lady Miriam…how well did you know her?'

'Just so so, I'd say. I met her mostly at the dining hall and the conversations were limited to the usual courtesies. "Good morning" and "how are you" and "it's such a lovely day, isn't it"— that kind of thing. Nothing much beyond that, I'm afraid.'

Thapa stared at Roy for a long time.

'But, you did find out something else about her?'

'You're right,' Roy admitted. 'It's just one day that we shared a long walk in the morning…to Pelling and back. She helped me out with the purchase of a few groceries.'

'Learnt anything significant about her?'

'Depends on what you consider to be significant. I'll tell you what I learnt. She talked about her past, her childhood. And how the church came as a big change in her life.'

Roy paused for a while, and then added, 'I believe that later on she became deeply attached to the church and was on the way to becoming a nun herself.'

'The arrival of the nun at the monastery isn't such a big surprise, then?'

'I'm not so sure about that. In the last five years that she had been coming to teach here, she's never had any visitor, especially from the church.'

'I see. Well, thank you very much for being so helpful. I'm sure you'll let me know if anything else comes to your mind.'

'Sure I will.' Roy got up from his chair and walked towards the door.

'I guess that's all for now.'

The murder attempt on the road and any possible connection of Miriam with the missing manuscript were carefully omitted. That would have been akin to letting a whole can of worms out. There was no mention of the affair with Lama Tenzing either.

After Roy left, Thapa asked for the guests and questioned them one by one. It was only when interrogating Billy did he come up with something that could be called a breakthrough. Billy had, apparently, taken pictures of Pierre's conversation with the nun the day before out of sheer fun. The cell phone he used had a powerful lens which enabled one to blow up the nun's face. This was the first authentic look at the murder suspect and Thapa had the nun's picture sent to all the police stations in Sikkim for urgent action.

When Roy came out of Miriam's room he found Pradyot busy taking pictures of the wall frescoes of the monastery.

'What's Tara doing on the walls of a Buddhist monastery?' Pradyot asked, curious.

'Tara is only a part of Tibetan Buddhism, which has a lot of Tantric influence in it. 'Will talk to you about it later. In the meantime we have work to do.'

They went down to the information desk in search of Lama Tashiding. The young lama was at his table, sorting out papers and files. But you could make out he was only going through the motions, endlessly arranging and rearranging the papers.

'Good afternoon.'

Tashiding looked up once to see who it was, then carried on with whatever he was doing.

'Good afternoon,' he mumbled.

'How long till your duties are over?'

Best to engage him in some inane conversation, Roy thought, to divert his mind.

The lama looked up at the wall clock and sighed.

'Another half an hour.'

'And then you will go for lunch?'

The lama nodded without looking up.

'But you don't have lunch at the regular dining hall?'

'No, we have a separate place for lunch.'

'The death of Miriam … it must have shaken you up very much.'

Tashiding stared hard at Roy.

'What do you think … we would be amused?'

Roy kept his silence.

'Do you realize that this is the first time that anything of this kind has ever happened in Dengziang? And, on top of it all, policemen coming and defiling our place.'

Roy knew he had hit a raw nerve there. He talked to the lama as gently as possible.

'This nun in the black outfit … I would imagine you've had a fair opportunity of observing her, haven't you?'

'I may have … so?'

'Would you like to describe her for me, please? You see, my problem is I haven't seen her at all. But you have. And before you say anything, I would like you to know that I believe every word that you've said so far. And will continue to do so.'

Tashiding looked up at Roy, at last a faint smile appearing on his face.

'Thank you, sir.'

'What was your initial reaction on seeing her?'

'Surprise…actually, more than surprise, shock!' his eyes widened in reaction. 'I wasn't really expecting a fully attired nun in front of me first thing in the morning. And I knew straightaway that she wasn't a tourist.'

'How did you figure that out?'

'You see…when the car stopped at the gate I happened to look out. The nun came out of the car, talked to the sentry and came straight to my table. I knew then she had come with a definite purpose.'

'Thank you…you're doing great, Lama Tashiding. Now describe her for me. Don't leave out anything…even if it strikes as trivial to you.'

'She came and enquired about Miriam. And…I was so startled, the papers slipped out of my hand and flew all over the floor. It was she who picked them up and put them back on the table, nicely arranged and all. And then…'

An embarrassed smile appeared on his face.

'And then…you noticed something?'

'Yes. She gave me a charming smile, and then…rearranged her clothes near her breasts, somewhat self-consciously, I thought.'

'A nun, self-conscious of her breasts!' Roy muttered to Pradyot. 'What will we have next!'

He turned back to Tashiding again.

'Would you describe her as a buxom lady?'

'Buxom?'

'Meaning…plump, round, fat.'

'Yes, yes. But, surprisingly, her face was sallow and hard.'

'That's interesting. What else? Anything unusual about her face? Maybe freckles…cut marks…anything out of the way?'

Tashiding stared at the wall clock, trying to remember.

'Her hair…'

'Yes, what about her hair?'

'The little bit of hair that I could see through the white cap was thick and matted. She had a very low forehead. As if…as if it was stuck on her head.'

'You mean…a wig?'

'Maybe…it just looked uncommon.' Tashiding said somewhat uncertainly. 'But then, some people have awfully thick, matted hair, you know. My maternal aunt, for instance.'

Roy suppressed a smile.

'And then…?'

'I gave her Miriam's room number. 'Instructed her as to how to find her way about. Actually, I volunteered to come with her. "No no…that won't be necessary," she said in a hurried manner.'

'That was all?'

'Yes. Then in the evening Miriam came down requesting me that the nun be allowed to stay the night with her.'

'After that you didn't get to see her till this morning?'

'That's right. She said she was leaving and asked me not to wake Miriam up too soon.'

'Why so?'

'She said they had chatted all night, that's why.'

'I see. Did she go out on foot? Or was there a car waiting for her?'

'No, there was no car. So she must have gone on foot. Oh yes! Now I remember. She had a mole…a pinkish brown lump of flesh on her chin. I also remember asking her to write a comment about her stay here in our guest book.'

'Oh! And did she oblige?'

'Yes, she did. She was rather amused at my request and said,

"Why not?"'

'Could we have a look at it, if you don't mind?'

'I don't see any harm in that.' Tashiding said enthusiastically. 'And since you tell me not to leave out even the trivial, I think she was wearing an unusual ring. I noticed it while she was writing in the book.'

'Unusual…in what sense?'

'It had a large star emblem, sort of a raised design, in place of a stone.'

By now he had forgotten the entire episode of being slighted by Inspector Thapa. He took the fat guest book out and opened the relevant page. Roy and Pradyot read the passage silently.

It said, *My stay here has been, indeed, most memorable. The food, though simple, was wholesome and delicious. So was the general service—full of courtesy and decorum. My only regret is that I have to leave today.*

Sister Cybil

Roy stared at the writing for a long time. He then took out his cell phone and sought Tashiding's permission to take a picture of the handwritten message.

'Anything the matter, sir?' Pradyot couldn't resist asking after they had left.

'Just a vague idea forming in my mind,' Roy said enigmatically.

What that idea was, Roy didn't bother to explain. As a matter of fact, Roy suddenly changed the topic of discussion to something totally different.

'The mole…Tashiding talked about the nun having a mole on her chin.'

'What about it?' Pradyot asked.

'The nun could very well be a fake,' Roy said, frowning.

'What makes you think so, sir?'

'You see, the mole is such a prominent thing. Anyone who takes a look at you…the first thing they notice is the mole on your face. The moment you remove it, you are a different person. So, if you're looking for the nun and you don't find the mole you immediately tend to look away. It's that simple,' Roy chuckled to himself. 'But, all the same, very very clever.'

Even after working for more than five years with this man, there were still occasions when Pradyot would be in absolute awe of him.

'I think the man we all are looking for is here.'

Pradyot turned around to find a car halting at the gate. It was the tomato-red taxi.

In Pelling, Norgay was popularly known as 'Mad Max'. Nobody drove his taxi as rashly, as ruthlessly and with such masterly control as he did. Negotiating sharp turns, steep climbs and hairpin bends was a piece of cake for him. All this he managed with great dexterity, just with his left hand. His right hand, alas, had been lost in his teens, while trying to make an improvised bomb.

As one would have expected, Max dressed flamboyantly. Black, wet-leather-look jacket; blue-tinted Wayfarer glasses; chunky wrist watch; heavy mountain boots. The boots, though, he wore not just as a fashion statement. Being short, those boots gave him a good two inches of extra height. Strands of jelled hair fell on his forehead à la Elvis.

When Tejpal picked him up from the town, he was having a 'drag' with a couple of 'gals'. But it was rudely interrupted by the cop who curtly ordered him to accompany him. It hurt his ego a great deal, especially being hauled up in front of the girls. But, being a smart chap, he knew how to turn adversity into an advantage.

So he turned around sweetly and said—'Anything to help the cops, man. Cause I've always been on the side of the law.'

To the girls he said with a wink, 'Don't go anywhere, sweethearts. I'm coming back soon.'

While Max drove at a sedate pace, dutifully following Tejpal's bike, his mind was working at lightning speed, trying to figure out why he was being picked up. Had they somehow got a sniff of his underhand drug deals? In that case, it was crucial for him to find out who might have snitched on him. Or was it something else? Not girls surely, for his sexual deviations, whatever they might be, were never performed without the girls' consent.

So, why were the cops interested in him? The reason manifested itself soon enough.

'What's your name?'

Max gave a considered reply. 'Norgay, sir.' He deliberately omitted mentioning his popular nickname. Thapa was known to be a cruel cop, who derived joy out of hurting people.

'Profession?'

'Taxi driver, sir.'

'That's obvious. What else do you do?'

'Nothing else, sir.'

'Then how did you manage to lose your right arm?'

Max shuffled his feet.

'It was an accident, sir.'

'Hmm…' Thapa nodded thoughtfully.' Making bombs…you call that an accident?'

That was the trouble with Inspector Thapa. He seemed to know everything about everyone in town.

'I was just watching, sir…not making it. The guy who was making it got blown up.'

Lie low, Max kept whispering to himself. He knew he hadn't

been hauled up for a misdemeanour committed nine years ago. It was simply Thapa's way of softening him up.

'Mad Max Norgay—that's what they call you, don't they? A name that you're so proud of. Do you know I can have your driving licence revoked immediately, if I wish to? Just like that!'

Thapa snapped his fingers to emphasize the point.

Max kept quiet, eyes lowered deferentially.

'So Max, where did you pick up this woman from, yesterday?'

'Which woman, sir?

Max was plainly foxed. He hadn't picked up any girl for his private pleasure yesterday.

'Think, Max…think. Which woman could it be?'

Thapa had converted the front office of the monastery into an interrogation chamber. He tapped his polished boots with a slim brown cane. Max knew it could be used any moment now, as a whip.

'Are you by any chance talking of the nun, sir? Max said in an inspired moment of mental deduction. 'The lady I brought over here yesterday?'

'Excellent, Max, excellent! Where did you pick her up from?'

'From the town, sir.'

'I know that, scoundrel!' Thapa brought down the cane resoundingly on the table. The audible swish in the air made Norgay flinch. 'Don't tax my patience, Max.'

Norgay closed his eyes. Any moment now the lashes would come raining down on his body.

'Where exactly did you pick her up from?'

'From the market, sir. Next to Jane Sherpa's junk jewellery shop.'

'No no…you aren't telling me the truth. Which hotel did you pick her up from?'

Thapa stared coldly at Norgay, saying nothing, doing nothing. He knew violence imagined could be far more potent than the actual act.

Norgay couldn't take the tension anymore. He fell down on his knees and pleaded for mercy.

'Upon god, sir…I'm telling you the truth. I picked her up from just outside the market. You could check with anyone there. Norgay was close to tears now.

'I don't like sissies.' He looked distastefully at Norgay's American diamond ear studs. '*Tu ladki banna chahta hai kya?*'

'I'll never wear them again, sir. Promise.'

'Hey!' Thapa held the well-oiled cane just under Norgay's chin and tilted it up. 'Look at me, bugger…look at me.'

Norgay was forced to look at those cold, ruthless eyes. Thapa kept staring at Norgay long and hard. Finally he said, 'I believe you. How did she make the payment? In dollars or in pounds?'

'In rupees, sir.'

So, that clever woman had converted her foreign exchange beforehand. The question was, where from? Gangtok or NJP? She could have converted the money from Kolkata, for all you know.

Thapa felt an insane rage welling inside, like milk on the boil. He wanted to punch, kick, smash, hurt, maim, even sodomize, someone…anyone, just to release his pent-up anger.

'Okay, Max, get up.'

Norgay gingerly got up from the floor, dusting his knees. Thapa rammed the cane stick into Norgay's body where it hurt the most, between his legs.

'This is what I want you to do. Go back to the township. Keep your eyes peeled and ears glued to the ground. I must find this woman. She couldn't have possibly vanished into thin air. Talk to your friends, fellow cabbies. Anyone, but anyone, who gives this woman a ride must immediately report back to me.'

Norgay nodded his head eagerly to whatever Thapa stated.

'Take this.' Thapa took out his personal card and gave it to Norgay. 'I must get this woman before nightfall. Do you understand?'

Norgay nodded again and quickly left the room. He could hardly contain himself anymore. The moment he was out of sight of the monastery, he stopped the car, let himself out and, standing in front of a bush, relieved himself with an audible sigh of relief.

Late in the day Roy received a message containing vital information. It came from St Mary's school in Coorg.

Earlier in the day Roy had sent a message to the school, enquiring whether there was actually any nun by the name of Sister Cybil with them. And, if so, whether she had in the recent past travelled to Pelling, a tourist spot in the eastern part of Sikkim. As an afterthought he had even sent the nun's specimen handwriting, as an attachment, to verify if it belonged to anyone in their institution.

Pat came the reply from the school secretary, saying, yes, there was indeed, a Sister Cybil amongst them. But no, she hadn't ventured out of town in the last three weeks. So there was no question of her being in Pelling. Coming to the handwritten specimen, the letter was unequivocal in maintaining that it bore no resemblance with that of anyone in their institution.

'You know what that means?' Roy showed the message on his cell phone to Pradyot. His assistant went over the letter carefully.

'That Sister Cybil of Pelling is most likely a fake?'

'Exactly. But what else does it tell us?'

Pradyot thought for a while, then shook his head.

'That the fake nun was very much aware of a genuine Sister Cybil in Coorg. And she manipulated that identity carefully so that there would be no questions raised in the monastery.'

Roy scratched his chin and felt the stubble. With everything happening in quick succession that morning, and last night's sleepless vigil watching the CCTV, he hadn't had time to shave.

'The obvious question, then, is if she is not the Mother Superior of the Coorg missionary school, who is she? If she is an imposter, which seems more than likely, why did Miriam agree to meet her? Why didn't she expose the fake Sister Cybil to the world?' Roy came up with a torrent of questions.

'Does it mean, Pradyot, that this nun had an unnatural hold on her? Did she know something from her past that Miriam didn't want anyone else to know? And that's how she was blackmailed into allowing the nun to stay the night with her?'

Roy kept scratching his chin irritably.

'And the most important question of them all, did the nun finally manage to get hold of what she came here for? Has she made off with the Issah manuscript?'

Pradyot thought for a while, then gave up.

'I have no idea, sir.'

'That makes two of us.'

After a while, a faint smile appeared on Roy's face.

'But, I think I know someone who does.'

His assistant looked thoroughly perplexed.

'You do?'

'Let's go, Pradyot. We will find him now.'

The whole morning Tenzing had been busy helping the boys with the shooting. In the last few days he had developed a fair idea, under the supervision of Pierre and his crew, of how to act in front of the camera. Paradoxical as it may sound, he had realized that the best way to get a good shot was to ignore the camera altogether and do your own thing.

In turn, Pierre and his company had found him to be more than useful. They realized that he was quick to grasp the basics of filmmaking and contributed handsomely by guiding the young lamas, some of them only five years old, to appear natural in front of the camera.

As for Tenzing and his boys, interactions with the outside world were transforming their lives in more ways than one could imagine. Miriam's coming down to Pelling each year to teach them English and Maths posed new challenges every day. Grappling with the verbs and genders, and the strange, often contradictory, pronunciations of English, more often than not, led to hilarious situations. The boys enjoyed it hugely. In addition, Miriam would often teach them History and Geography, opening up new vistas, new horizons.

To top it all, the experience of being a part of filmmaking—to them it was an escape to fantasy land. It was a welcome respite from the daily drudgery of having to memorize pages of Buddhist scriptures, which they were made to read aloud in a sing-song manner every morning. They were simply awestruck by the mad energy with which the crew worked; setting up the lights and stands, fixing the bouncing boards and reflectors, laying the tracks for a trolley shot, rolling the camera. And at the end of it all, three magical words—lights, camera, action.

The young lamas simply loved it.

That day when they returned from the shoot, initially no one told them anything about Miriam's death. They knew how much the children would be affected by the news. Miriam was the most popular teacher they'd ever had.

As Lama Phunsok called Tenzing over to his room and gently broke the news to him the young lama just couldn't believe his ears. How could that be? She had taken classes with them only the day before. As the class monitor, it was his duty to collect the exercise books from the rest of the students and hand them over to her. As he did so, their hands had touched inadvertently. The contact had been like an electric shock, setting his pulses racing. His face had looked flushed. At the same time he had felt a certain tautness in the lower part of his body that rendered him virtually immobile.

'Look at me,' she had whispered to him so that nobody else could hear. And he had looked up at her face stealthily, totally hypnotized by the pink lips breaking into a pearly smile. She seemed to be speaking to him, but he didn't follow a single word of it.

'I feel the same way too.'

It was as if he had been transported to cloud nine.

'Are you all right, my boy?' Phunsok enquired. All of a sudden, Tenzing looked rather pale to him.

'No, sir. It's just that … it's so difficult to believe she's no more.' Tenzing couldn't bring himself to say the word 'dead'.

'Go to her room. Her body … I mean she's still there. But any moment now the police will come and take her away for post-mortem.'

'Post-mortem! Meaning, they will cut her up?'

'I'm afraid so. It's the normal police procedure in case of abnormal deaths.'

'Her death … was … abnormal?' he asked haltingly.

'Go now, before it's too late.'

In a rare moment of insight it had dawned on him that Tenzing's feelings for Miriam could be something much more than the normal adoration for one's favourite teacher. As a practising lama, Phunsok might be sworn to celibacy for life, but he couldn't be so insensitive as to deny Tenzing a last meeting, as it were, with Miriam.

Eyes blinded by tears, Tenzing rushed out of the room and ran across the open courtyard towards the guest house. The police guard posted at Miriam's door barred his entry, but at Roy's request let him in.

'Please grant him a moment's privacy,' said Roy. 'After all, she was their favourite teacher.'

The guard looked at Tenzing, then at the body lying on the bed, and thought for a while.

'But no touching,' he wagged his finger at the young lama before leaving the room.

Roy, too, stepped out, gently closing the door behind him.

At last Tenzing was alone with her. He wiped the tears from his eyes so he could see her properly. He brought his face close to hers, taking, the paleness of her lips, the lack of colour on her cheeks. He so dearly wanted to kiss her, hold her in his arms and feel his body against hers. He looked back at the door. There was no one there. But death had now put an immeasurable distance between the two of them. And there was no way he could breach it.

He sank to his knees and hid his face on the bed, next to her body, and wept inconsolably.

Just then a shadow passed across the bed and Tenzing realized someone had entered the room. He lifted his blood-shot eyes and turned around to find Roy standing behind him.

'Tenzing, it may not seem to be the best moment to talk, but may I have a few words with you?'

A gentle, comforting hand came down and rested on his shoulder. The boy still remained on his knees, his face buried in bed, weeping, his body shaking silently. He so desperately wanted to touch her hands, hug her and implore her to come back to life, saying, 'You cannot just leave me like this…it's not fair, not fair at all.'

Time stopped still. It seemed like an eternity. But then the minute passed. Tenzing rose on his feet and faced Roy.

'It's no use, saying, "I understand how you feel." For nobody will ever understand the extent of pain that you are going through just now. So I won't even try to console you.'

Roy remained silent for a while.

'But I need to talk to you, and it's urgent. You see…she didn't die a natural death. We think it's murder.'

The boy cringed visibly, as if someone had just whipped him.

'What…what are you saying?' He looked down at the prone body on the bed, then looked back at Roy.

'She's been murdered?'

Roy simply nodded his head.

'In a short while the police will come and take her body away. They will conduct a post-mortem on her. And they will find that she was first made to drink a beverage that was spiked with some kind of a drug to make her fall unconscious and, then, throttled to death.'

'No, this can't be.'

The boy's face was contorted with pain. Then suddenly he went still.

'Is it that woman…the nun who came in yesterday?'

'So it would seem. There was no one else in the room last night.'

'Where's she now?' the boy's face had gone blank.

Roy was sure a rage was blazing inside him. And if, by any chance, he had found her now, she would have died a most violent death in his hands.

'She left the monastery in the morning. The police are looking for her everywhere. But, till now, she has remained untraceable.'

The boy's hands turned into fists.

'Listen, Tenzing, there's no time for anger…or for revenge. We have to act now. This nun…she came to stay with her for a specific purpose. It might seem pure conjecture, but she had probably given Miriam a task…to remove something from the monastery by stealth; perhaps a secret document, a rare manuscript. Do you know anything about it?

'N…no.' The boy hesitated for a fraction of a second.

'Don't try to hide anything from me. If you speak the truth, it would be easier for us to catch her. You want that, don't you?'

'No…nothing transpired really.' His whole body heaved, though he may not have been aware of it.

'But, she did ask you to do something for her?'

His eyes were closely watching the boy's face now.

The boy nodded silently.

'She asked you to get something from the underground vault?'

The boy nodded again.

'Did you retrieve it for her?'

'No, I told her it would be the most difficult thing to do, virtually impossible. She thought for a while. And then she said it was all right if I couldn't do it. She won't hold it against me.'

'Just that! Nothing else?'

'Nothing else, sir. I'm telling you the truth.' His voice was drained of all emotions now.

There were sounds of heavy boots approaching the room.

'Leave now. They've come to take her away.'

Quietly Tenzing bent down to kiss her on the forehead and left the room.

When Roy went downstairs for dinner that night the dining hall wore a gloomy look. His steps slowed down a trifle, as he glanced at the empty Table Number Two. Miriam wouldn't come and sit down there anymore. Nor would anybody else, in the near future. Everyone knew and liked her so much.

As he crossed Table Number Three, Pierre barely looked up. He mumbled something. At Table Number Four Billy didn't stretch out his huge paw to bar Roy's passage. He didn't even look up, but seemed to concentrate on a notebook, scribbling down something with furious concentration. Table Number Five, usurped these days by the 'silent' duo, was empty that night. But Roy chose not to sit there. He sat at the extreme, gloomiest corner of the hall.

When food was served, he just toyed with it. He felt no hunger. After a while, he got up from the table, mumbled a 'goodbye' to no one in particular, and left. On his way upstairs he stopped at the ground floor landing and looked towards the verandah. A policeman was posted outside Miriam's door. So her personal stuff was presumably still there. Who would collect them now? Had Lama Phunsok instructed someone to inform Miriam's household and, perhaps, the school where she had taught? By her own admission, she had lived the last two years of her life at the school itself.

Once upstairs, he stood at the balcony and looked at the empty chairs. Here, only the day before, Miriam had spent an entire afternoon chatting with the nun. He entered his room and stood in the middle for a while, not knowing what to do. He then did the most uncharacteristic thing by taking out the whisky bottle from the suitcase and pouring himself generous measures from it to get himself punch-drunk.

Knowing that now nothing much was likely to happen, he no longer sat at the table to scan the CCTV screens. Miriam was dead. His period of watch was over.

But he was wrong.

Next morning he was woken up by a swarm of bumblebees. For a minute he couldn't figure out what was happening. And then suddenly he knew what it was. It was the children, the little lamas who were wailing outside in the courtyard. He cursed himself for getting drunk last night and ran out to the balcony. What he saw happening out there was a theatre of the absurd, reminding him of Ionesco's *Rhinoceros*. The children ran blindly all about the courtyard, often bumping against each other, in a state of frenzy. He saw Lama Tashiding and Chorten trying their best to pacify them. But the children simply wouldn't relent. If anything, their cries kept rising in a crescendo, till it actually hurt his eardrums. Through all this shrieking and howling, Roy could vaguely make out one word, one name actually—that of Tenzing's.

What about Tenzing? That's right. Why wasn't he there in the courtyard with the rest of the boys? He was their warden, after all.

When Roy reached Tenzing's room, adjacent to the children's dormitory, he found the latter in a pool of blood. Someone had slit his throat almost into half. Tenzing must have been fast asleep when the attack was made, for there was no resistance, no fight from his side.

As a rule, it was Tenzing's duty to wake the kids up at 5.30 a.m. every morning. But that day he had failed to do so. By 6 a.m., many of the kids had woken up out of sheer habit and were quite perplexed to find that Tenzing was not there. Two of the kids had then gathered enough courage to go and knock at Tenzing's door. Finding no response from inside, they had pushed the door in. It was Tenzing's clear instruction that, should any of the younger boys wake up scared at night, his door was always open for them. He was like their big brother, their knight in shining armour, protecting them from all the evil jinns that roamed about the nocturnal world.

At first the children couldn't make out anything clearly. The curtains across the solitary window in the room were tightly drawn. But once their eyes got used to the darkness, they found Tenzing soaked in blood. It was then that they threw the door wide open and ran out, shrieking and howling. The lad who had protected them for so long would now come back to haunt them forever in their nightmares.

The doctor who had been called in from Pelling pronounced Tenzing dead. Cause of death—infliction of injury to the body with a sharp object, most probably a knife or a razor, leading to extensive bleeding and eventual death.

The doctor was smart enough not to touch the body, or any other object in the room.

When most of the people had left, Roy came back to the room and looked around. Tenzing's room had not just been searched, his belongings had been ransacked. The few clothes that he had were all strewn across the floor. His religious books were in shambles, ripped apart with a vengeance.

Roy came back to Tenzing's body and bent down to look at the face. He sniffed audibly a couple of times. Wasn't there a familiar smell coming from the face? What was it? And then it struck him. It was chloroform, of course. He looked up at the window. It didn't have a grill. So someone had slipped into the room through the window last night and pressed a chloroformed handkerchief to Tenzing's face to knock him unconscious.

The assassin didn't know, of course, that the door wasn't locked at all.

That morning Chief Inspector Thapa was conducting office from home. He had a terrible cold that made him shake and shiver, in spite of being wrapped in a heavy blanket. He sneezed uncontrollably. His nose ran like a leaking faucet. Every now and then he would reach for the packet of tissue papers, held by an ardali or attendant, and blow into one loudly, sounding like a neighing horse. Crumpled and soiled tissue papers lay strewn all over the expensive wooden floor.

In Pelling, this was serious news. For, in the last thirty years, no one had ever seen Thapa report sick. He had the constitution of an ox. Short, stocky, barrel-chested, he was, in his youth, a state-ranking pugilist. But last night something must have happened that didn't quite agree with him. For the life of him he couldn't figure out what. Perhaps, he had put too much ice in his drinks. But then, he had been drinking whisky on the rocks for as long as he could remember.

Maybe age was, finally, catching up with him.

It was barely 9 a.m. But already the key members of his team were all assembled in his spacious drawing room. Tejpal, his assistant, stood just behind him, hands folded deferentially, head slightly inclined towards Thapa to be able to catch his boss's rasping whisper. Ram Bahadur stood like a statue by his side, holding the wad of tissue papers. Gurung manned the entrance door. Two more policemen stood at attention, just in case they were needed for anything.

Thapa sat on a high-backed chair, his bare feet submerged in a pale blue, round plastic tub, full of scalding hot water. From time to time, he sipped a steaming, dark and menacing-looking concoction from a large porcelain mug. Kamala, his wife, had lovingly prepared it by boiling Assam tea with various herbs, including fresh tulsi leaves, cardamom powder, cloves and crushed ginger. It tasted horrible. But it was working. Already, he felt his head clearing.

One by one the informers filed in.

'Yes...Mad Max?' Thapa looked up at Norgay with blood-shot eyes. 'What have you got to report?'

Norgay was still dressed like the day before. The faux black leather jacket still shone with metal studs. The chunky wrist watch still adorned his wrists. And the fake mountain boots still gave him the extra two inches of height. Only the American diamond ear studs were missing. Norgay had no intention of incurring the wrath of the Chief Inspector again.

'Sir,' he chose to fix his eyes at a point about six inches above the inspector's head, 'the nun that you spoke of isn't here.'

Thapa made a big show of looking searchingly around him in the room.

'Yeah...profound observation, Max! I can see that she isn't here.'

'I didn't mean it that way, sir.' Norgay chose not to react to Thapa's jibe. 'She isn't here...in Pelling.'

'Hmm, never short of confidence...that's what I particularly like about you, Max.' Thapa reached for another tissue paper from Ram Bahadur's hand and sneezed into it.

'But, tell me Max...what makes you so confident about the nun? That she's not here?'

'I've made my enquiries, sir.'

Indeed, Norgay had. He knew every nook and corner in Pelling like the back of his hand. And he had scoured every one of those hideouts, including the lone house of disrepute in the town, without finding any trace of the nun.

'Okay,' Thapa looked speculatively at Norgay. 'I buy your statement, for the time being.'

Norgay heaved a visible sigh of relief.

'But don't go anywhere,' warned the inspector. 'I'm not through with you yet. Singh…get him a cup of tea and something to munch.'

Havildar Singh left the room to do the needful.

'Who's next?' Thapa turned around and looked at Tejpal.

'Sir, both Nandu and Jacob are here. Shall I bring them in?'

Thapa nodded. Havildar Gurung went out and came back in a short while, accompanied by two nondescript chaps. Thapa readily recognized Nandu, the older of the two.

'How are you, Nandu? *Sab theek hai?*'

Nandu felt immensely flattered that the Chief Inspector not only remembered his face, but even his name.

Nandu was a jack of all trades. He had started out life as a lowly porter, but had, through sheer diligence, picked up other competencies as well. So that now, he was a full-fledged mason, electrician, carpenter and a reasonably good plumber as well. There were few homes in Pelling that he didn't have access to; excellent qualifications for an informer.

The other person Thapa didn't know was Jacob.

'So this is Jacob. What does he do for a living?' Thapa gave the newcomer a cold stare.

'Works in a travel agency named Sunshine. It's in the main marketplace, sir.' Tejpal spoke on behalf of Jacob.

'Good.' Thapa nodded imperceptively. 'Gives him access to all the tourists in town.'

'So, Nandu…do you have a picture of the nun in question?'

Tejpal had made a number of printouts from the picture of the nun, provided by Billy, and had it distributed to all the important areas in Pelling. There was reason to hope that at least someone would be able to spot her.

'Yes, sir,' replied Nandu. He fished out a picture from his

pocket and showed it to the inspector.

'Have you seen her anywhere before?'

'No, I don't think so.' He kept staring at the picture for a long time. 'I'm sure I would've recognized the face if I had seen her, what with that prominent mole on her chin.'

'You, Jacob?' Thapa asked the other person.

Jacob shook his head in answer.

'I say, Tejpal, this is absolutely crazy!'

'What is, sir?' Tejpal wasn't quite sure what his boss had found crazy that particular moment.

'Don't talk like an imbecile!' Thapa exploded.

As it is, he was a man with a quick temper. And now, the lack of any progress in the Miriam murder case made him boil with rage.

'Here's this European nun who comes to Dengziang Monastery, stays a night there, killing a woman and walks away in broad daylight. And no one has seen her before, or since then? I'm asking how's that possible? How can that woman vanish into thin air?'

No one in the room had an answer to that.

'Tejpal,' Thapa kicked the plastic tub with a vengeance, splashing water all over the floor, 'ask someone to take it away. It's gone cold anyway.'

'Shall I replace the tub with fresh hot water?'

Thapa shook his head.

'Some more herbal tea, then?'

'No, I don't need anything, from you or anybody else, Tejpal,' Thapa shouted back at his assistant with uncalled-for vehemence. 'I just need time to think.'

He got up from his chair and started pacing about the room on bare feet, looking quite a sight. Part of the blanket trailed far behind him like a flowing wedding gown. A few of the crumpled tissue papers lying on the floor got stuck to the blanket, making them look like decorative flowers, accentuating the look of the wedding gown. If anybody in the room found it funny, he certainly didn't show it.

Suddenly Thapa stopped dead in front of Tejpal and started giggling uncontrollably. He giggled so much that tears came out of his eyes.

'Shhitt!' he repeated the word coarsely a few times. 'How could I miss it? It was staring at me all this time and I never even noticed it!'

Nobody dared to ask what he should have seen right from the beginning.

'How stupid of me and how clever of the woman!'

Tejpal held his breath, knowing the explanation would come soon enough.

'That bloody woman! Either she's no nun, or she shed the nun's clothes the moment she was out of sight. And all this while we were looking for a white woman in a black cassock. How easily she had us fooled! Ha ha ha!'

Thapa finally collapsed on the chair.

'Tejpal, Singh, Gurung, Max, Nandu and you, Jacob!' Thapa tapped the travel agent on the chest with the point of his polished cane. 'Get out of this place without any more delay. God knows… by now she might even be out of Pelling and out of our reach. But let's try and nab this bitch. Anyone of you sees a European middle-aged woman anywhere in Pelling, report it to me or Tejpal immediately. Tejpal, you have the authority to stop any such woman and have her brought to the police station for further questioning. Is that understood? Now leave… all of you.'

'Yes, sir.'

'See you at the station in half an hour.'

Tejpal rounded up his men and left hurriedly in the Jeep. Nandu and Jacob left the way they had come...through the back door.

That morning a pall of gloom descended upon the monastery. Miriam's unnatural death had generally been regarded as shocking. But, all things said and done, she was still an outsider. Whereas Tenzing's murder was an invasion of the sanctum sanctorum, the inner circle. It was like a sucker punch in the solar plexus, knocking the very breath out of the inmates of the monastery.

The senior lamas were all there, filing in near the children's dorm. Tenzing's room was at the rear end. Since it was so tiny, everyone could not be accommodated inside. So, some of the lamas had perforce to stand outside, in the sun.

It was a brilliant morning. A blue sky shimmered, without a single cloud. Kites flew in concentric circles, occasionally breaking tedium by chasing each other, indulging in spectacular swoops and dives like pairs of well-rehearsed ballet artists. In the manicured gardens of the monastery, so lovingly tended by the little lamas, geraniums and petunias were in full bloom. Nature, it seemed, could be cruelly forgetful of the dead.

Lama Phunsok had actually broken down. He sat on a small folding chair at the head of Tenzing's bed, his bloodshot eyes unable to contain the tears anymore.

'He was just a tiny little boy when his father brought him to our monastery, smaller than anybody else in the children's dormitory. And I said to his father, "Isn't he too young to come here? Bring him back after a year or two, if you must." His father smiled his quiet little smile. "No sir," he said, "my little one's ready for the journey."' Lama Phunsok said to no one in particular.

'Eleven years have gone by...and look how big he is now. So strong, yet so light of feet. Always a smiling face. Always eager to run your errands.'

Phunsok looked fondly at Tenzing, then shuddered at the sight of the slit throat. He was desperately trying to come to terms with the horrific act.

'Someone killed him. But who? Who could've possibly wanted to kill him, I ask?'

No one answered.

'So he must have had an enemy? That's so hard to believe. Tenzing had an enemy. Chornum, can you believe it?'

Lama Chornum stood mute by his side and shook his head. He, too, was close to tears.

'All the years of training, all the goodness and obedience taught and learnt, all the respect for one's elders...he had it all. Then why should anyone want to kill him?'

A long minute of silence ensued.

'Truly, we live in a vile world today,' Phunsok shook his head, unable to carry on anymore. His words had dried up at last. But the flow of tears hadn't.

He got up stiffly from the chair with the help of others, as though his legs were unable to support him anymore. In the last one hour he had grown older by ten years.

'Let me know if I'm needed for anything. I can't take this.' So saying, he left the room, and would have surely tripped on the door sill hadn't one of the younger lamas caught him just in time. After a while Lama Chornum also left.

But the most devastated by this death were the kids. They were simply inconsolable. Normally so jovial and carefree, they had stopped eating and playing. It was as if all life had been drained out of them. Seeing their condition, the senior lamas decided on sending them back to their respective homes for the time being. Being with the family might help assuage their pain.

And then there were the unexpected visitors. But, if you thought about it, maybe they were not so unexpected, after all. Miriam's father came from Coorg along with his eldest daughter, Julia. She had been the closest to Miriam during the latter's early years.

Tenzing's family came too. They lived only a few kilometres away from the monastery, in the outskirts of the town. Tenzing's mother didn't utter a single word during the visit, remaining stoical, without tears. Lord Buddha had taken her child away, first to the monastery, and now to the heaven to reside with Him. It was only when she was face to face with her son's body that she attempted to take him in her arms. She was led away from the room by her youngest son. It was Johnny, the eldest one of the family, who wept bitterly. It was sheer accident, he said, that he was the first born. It could have easily been the other way round. And then, he would've been the one to be sent to the monastery to become a monk. Johnny's son, Toto, seeing his favourite uncle lying in a pool of blood howled so much that he had to be carried away. Johnny recalled how only a few days ago Tenzing had come home to celebrate Toto's birthday and lifted him up in air—an act that delighted the boy more than anything else. Lara stood silently near the door, eyes brimming with tears.

As for Miriam's father and sister, they were taken to Miriam's room and asked to take charge of her belongings. He picked up each and every article belonging to Miriam lovingly, putting as many of them as he could inside the suitcase. The rest, he made

into a neat little bundle and gave it to the monastery, to be given
away to a charitable home.

Later they went to the lone morgue in Pelling to see
Miriam. In the ice-cold room Miriam's body was brought out of
the metallic shelf, her naked body covered with a single white
sheet. The coroner removed part of the cover to reveal a pale
blue face as if made of translucent glass. Her body had been cut
from chest downwards in a long vertical line up to her abdomen.
They had obviously wanted to verify if she had been poisoned
or drugged, prior to being throttled to death. Later on, they had
loosely stitched her up with a large needle, so part of her flesh
still showed through. The sight made Julia run out of the room
and puke.

Just as Phunsok was crossing the courtyard towards his living
quarters, a police Jeep roared into the monastery compound and
screeched to a halt near the children's dorm. Inspector Thapa
stepped out of the front seat of the Jeep, his signature brass-
knobbed baton in one hand and a wad of tissue papers in the
other. He was closely followed by Tejpal and two other constables.
It was apparent that Thapa knew the layout of the monastery well,
for he walked straight past the dorm, up the two steps that led to
the warden's room.

Seeing him, the monks stepped aside, making room for him.
Thapa halted at the door, taking note of everything. The deep gash
on Tenzing's throat was visible from a distance. As also the fact
that there had been no struggle between the killer and his victim.
It could mean one of two things—that the killer and the victim
knew each other beforehand; or that the victim was fast asleep

when the murder was committed. From the corner of his eye he also spotted Roy in the background and permitted a ghost of a smile in acknowledgement.

'Can we have the room cleared out, please?' he said with a casual glance towards the monks.

'No offence meant. I will call you as and when required.'

The monks started filing out one by one.

'I hope nothing in the room has been tampered with. And that includes the body.'

'Yes,' said Lama Chorten before leaving.

Thapa stepped forward to stand next to the body, so he could inspect it better. Something that he saw must have intrigued him, for he bent low to have a closer look at the wound.

'Hmm,' he nodded to himself. 'The cut couldn't have been made with an ordinary dagger or a knife. Could be something special...maybe a Swiss knife?'

He turned enquiringly at Roy as if the latter was part of his entourage. Roy merely shrugged in response. The thought hadn't occurred to him.

'The place has been ransacked and there is no sign of struggle either. Was he drugged, then?'

'Possible,' Roy said quietly. 'I thought there is a faint smell of chloroform about him.'

Thapa bent close to Tenzing's face and sniffed.

'Why!' he gave a surprised look at Roy. 'You could be right.'

His nose started running again. Maybe he was allergic to corpses. He took out a tissue paper and blew hard into it. Then, not finding a place where he could dump it, he put it into Tejpal's hand. If Tejpal was discomfited by this act, he didn't show it.

'Incidentally, Mr Roy, the initial autopsy report has just arrived. Any guesses on what it might contain?'

'Residue of sleeping pills crushed and skilfully mixed into a health drink?'

Thapa threw a quick look at Roy.

'But what made you think it was sleeping pills, and not poison?'

Roy smiled briefly before answering.

'Signs of struggle...Miriam was most likely throttled to death. Had she been poisoned there wouldn't have been any need for that.'

'My my!' A grudging admiration appeared on Thapa's face.

'A veritable Sherlock Holmes.'

Thapa, it seemed, was incapable of admiring anything without sarcasm. He remained silent for a while, perhaps deciding on how much to confide in Roy.

'I have to admit that your guess is by and large correct. Actually, sleeping pills in a powdered form were administered to a malt drink, not poison. She died of asphyxiation.'

Roy looked at Thapa, but didn't comment.

'What really bugs me is this. I know there are important differences between the two murders.'

Thapa came and stood in front of Roy.

'In Miriam's case it was sleeping pills, followed by choking to death. In the young monk's case, whatever his name was...'

'Tenzing.' Roy prompted softly.

'Yes yes...Tenzing. In Tenzing's case it was by slitting his throat with a sharp weapon. But, in spite of the differences in modus operandi, I think there is a definite connection between the two. What say you?'

'Perhaps. Two murders in quick succession, at the same place—it couldn't be just a coincidence,' Roy conceded.

Roy had to remain guarded about how much to tell Thapa. No

matter what, he couldn't disclose the secret of the missing Issah manuscript. He was honour-bound to Lama Phunsok to keep it under wraps.

'Perhaps?' Thapa gave him a quizzical look. 'Because you think that the nun, or whosoever that woman is, couldn't have entered the monastery and committed the murder all by herself?'

Roy gave him a short nod. That would be the most expedient answer perhaps.

'And the knife…' Thapa blew his nose again. His snub nose was looking increasingly red now. 'If it is a Swiss knife at all, it could very much be the handiwork of a foreigner. An authentic Swiss army knife is not easily available in our country. So, finally we come back to the nun, don't we?'

Thapa was increasingly making Roy a party to his discussions.

'Oh! And the nun might not be a nun at all. Because our men haven't been able to find any trace of her. So she could be any foreigner, masquerading as a nun. I thought I would let you know that.'

'Thanks,' Roy muttered.

'Two murders committed in the same monastery…it can't be that the monks know nothing about it. So we need to talk to Lama Phunsok, Tshering and Chornum. Care to come with me, Roy?'

Roy gently declined the offer.

'I have some private business that needs urgent attention.'

The first thing that Roy did after entering his room was to playback last night's CCTV footage, especially those cameras that covered the entrance and the courtyard of the monastery. Anybody wanting to approach the children's dormitory had to pass these two cameras. Yet, even after repeatedly watching the footage, he couldn't detect any movement there. No woman in black cassocks had slid past the entrance gate or stealthily crossed the courtyard.

That's surprising. Roy frowned absentmindedly at the screen. Could there be a back entrance to the monastery, then? Or had the nun scaled the boundary walls? Could a dowdy-looking, middle-aged woman be capable of that? Frankly, he didn't know.

A little later Pradyot called up to report on the nun. He had visited each and every hotel and guesthouse in Pelling in search of a middle-aged Caucasian woman and found none. The only person who came close to matching that description was an English lady who was visiting Pelling with her husband and little daughter. By no stretch of imagination could she be construed as the one they were looking for.

At 3 o'clock in the afternoon he received an SMS from Dr Adinath Goswami. The cryptic message had asked Roy to be prepared with a copy of the nun's handwriting in half an hour's time.

Dr Adinath Goswami happened to be the most famous graphologist in Kolkata and a personal friend of Roy's. The detective had actually enlisted the former's help in an earlier case that had helped him nab a diabolically clever murderer. When he had seen the nun's handwritten note at Tashiding's office, the first thing that had crossed his mind was to send it across to Dr Goswami for an analysis of the writer's character. Which is why he had taken the photograph of the nun's handwriting in his high resolution cell phone camera and mailed it to his graphologist friend.

At 3.30 p.m. sharp, the call came through.

'Roy?'

'Yeah, I've got the text in front of me. Frankly, what do you make of it?'

'Hi hi hi hi…' Roy heard chuckles from the other end.

'What's so funny?'

'The most interesting case! The handwriting you sent me yesterday…very interesting indeed.'

Dr Goswami chuckled some more.

Roy waited patiently for the graphologist to come to the point.

'First of all, a disclaimer. It might sound somewhat deflating to you, but the truth is there is no such thing as, quote unquote, "murderer's handwriting".'

The words sounded like damp squib to Roy.

'Anyone is capable of committing murder under certain extreme circumstances.'

'So…what are you trying to say?'

'What I'm telling you is this. A handwriting specimen can help evaluate a crime-prone personality. But then, this has to match the circumstantial evidence of motive and the writer's personality.'

It sounded all gibberish to Roy.

'Can we come to the point?' he said a little impatiently.

'That's exactly what I'm trying to do, my dear fellow, if you will allow me to. In case of domestic murders…it's mostly done by ordinary people. Here, sudden bursts of uncontrolled anger with impulsive ruthlessness may be discerned.'

Roy let out an exasperated sigh. Never mind the urgency of the matter, Dr Goswami was going to take his own sweet time.

'Listen…do you…'

'Don't interrupt…in case of rape and murder, unnaturally strong sexual desire, along with a crime-prone character may be present. And in case of cold-blooded murder as seen in the case of a psychopath, the writing may reveal cold emotions, lack of any sense of guilt, extreme tension, anger, pent-up emotional rage. Along with these primary features, a pleasant approachable behaviour on the surface, hiding inner aggression, may also be present.'

Dr Goswami droned on and on.

'Now, if we imagine the present case to belong to the last category, the handwriting shows the following features.'

Suddenly, Roy's senses became all alert. The last mentioned symptoms seemed to match that of the nun very closely.

'Roy, are you there? You seem to have gone very quiet.'

'On the contrary, I'm all ears.'

'Well, the first point it reveals is fluctuating pressure during writing, whereby some letters appear deep and some letters shallow. Now, look up the nun's handwriting. Where she writes "the food, though simple"…the lettering is particularly deep with the word "simple", while in case of the following two words, "has been", the pressure point is rather shallow.'

Roy looked up the nun's handwriting and found that it made perfect sense.

'It reveals the writer's fluctuating emotional state, swinging between two extremely vulnerable positions like a pendulum. The second point…'

Roy could make out that Dr Goswami was reading it out to him from a written note.

'If you look at the handwriting, the upright letter formation shows that her head rules over her heart. Also, a strong self-control that is not shaken on the face of extreme aggression. The third point to notice is the appearance of thread formations, revealing capacity for manipulating others to serve one's own purpose.' Exactly what the nun had done with Miriam.

'Downward strokes, thickening at the bottom, suggest rage and aggression, and when this is combined with horizontal club strokes as can be seen in crossing out of the letter "t" and "f", it reveals pure brutality. Most interestingly, garland type "m" and "n" shows her odd personality. Maybe she is a female with a very strong manly disposition, or a man with strong feminine tendencies.'

The last line was the clincher. But Roy still wanted to be sure.

'So what's your considered opinion?'

'I cannot say this with absolute certainty. However, there is a strong possibility that the writer of this text might not be a woman at all, but a man; a man whose brutal nature is carefully hidden by an apparently friendly exterior and curiously girlish traits.'

Roy thanked Dr Goswami profusely for the latter's interpretation of the nun's handwriting.

Everything was falling into place now. This was why Lama Tashiding had found the nun self-consciously adjusting her clothes around her breasts during their first meeting. Because she wasn't a woman at all. When he picked up Lama Tashiding's papers from the floor, he thought that the position of his artificial breasts might have shifted and it might get noticed by Lama Tashiding. Also, no wonder Tashiding had found the nun to have a deep, husky voice.

A brief smile appeared on Roy's face. The man masquerading as the nun, whoever he might be, had done a remarkable impersonation of Mrs Doubtfire.

Roy called up Pradyot and confided in him regarding his findings.

'It seems that in trying to catch the nun we have been drawn into a wild goose chase all this time.'

'I'm not sure if I understand you, sir.'

'The person we are looking for might not be a woman at all.'

'You are joking, surely?'

'I've never been more earnest in my life.'

Pradyot remained silent. Actually, his mind was racing back to an insignificant incident of that morning. Or, what he thought to be insignificant at the time. An incident that had taken place at the reception desk of the hotel as he was coming out of the dining room after breakfast.

'Pradyot, are you there?'

'Yes, sir,' he apologized to Roy. 'Can I be excused for a minute?'

'Yes, of course! But, what's it about?'

But by then Pradyot had disconnected the phone. He hurriedly locked the room behind him and ran down the staircase as fast as he could. The receptionist was busy watching something on his cell phone.

'Hello…' Pradyot cleared his throat loudly.

'Yes?' responded the receptionist, his eyes still on the cell phone.

'Can I have a look at your register book please?'

'May I know what this is about?'

He gave Pradyot a bored look.

'It's not our usual practice, sir.'

Pradyot gave him a thin smile, reached over the counter and grabbed the receptionist by the collar, pulling him up till the latter's face was level with his own.

'Then make it so.'

He thrust the police ID card in front of the receptionist.

'Do you see this?'

The grip on the collar was so severe that the receptionist had problems breathing.

'Yes, sir…' he said with much difficulty. 'If you will only relax the grip a little, sir, so I could breathe.'

'Good.' He let go of the grip so suddenly that the receptionist toppled over backwards, falling on the floor. The man got up hurriedly and produced the register book on the counter with remarkable dexterity.

Pradyot sifted through the book quickly to arrive at the last few pages of entry. His eyes ran down the guest list to rest upon a particular name—Antonio Vitolo. Arrived from Kolkata. Going back to Kolkata.

'Did you check his passport?'

'Yes, sir.'

'Nationality?'

'From Italy, I think.'

Pradyot reached out with his long arm and snatched the cell phone from the reception desk, taking a peek at it.

'This is what happens when you are watching porn…on duty.'

The man behind the counter looked away guiltily.

'Now be a good boy,' Pradyot pulled the guy up by his tie, 'and show me the copy of his passport.'

The man looked at him, surprised.

'Don't look so naïve. You're supposed to keep a Xerox copy of each guest's ID, aren't you?'

The receptionist meekly nodded his head and started looking for the copy of Antonio's passport. He went through the drawers and the various files, but still couldn't find it.

'I…I must have misplaced it somewhere.'

'How convenient!' Pradyot leaned over the counter to come face to face with the receptionist. 'I think you deliberately forgot to make a copy of his passport in lieu of money.'

'No no sir…it's not like that. It's just that I can't remember where I kept it.'

The man winced in anticipation of another physical onslaught.

Pradyot casually glanced at the register book to take a look at Mr Vitolo's date of arrival at the hotel. It was the same day that Sister Cybil had showed up at Dengziang Monastery in the afternoon.

Inspector Thapa, instead of going back to his residence, as his ill health would have warranted, returned straight to the police station. He wasn't used to failure. And if you could condone his fiery temper, he wasn't such a bad cop at all. So, his apparent failure to make any significant progress in the case of the vanishing nun made him furious with himself.

Also, the problem of the running nose had eased somewhat. So, he had stopped littering the office with crumpled and soggy tissue papers. But he still carried with him a bottle of nose drops for his clogged nose, which necessitated him to make frequent neighing sounds, just so that he could breathe.

'This is blasphemous! Here I am in my own beat, surrounded by assistants, constables, havildars and a group of informers who are supposed to have their eyes and ears glued to the ground. And yet, I haven't been able to catch one single fat middle-aged woman.'

He kicked back his chair with the heels of his shoes and started prowling behind the table like a caged animal.

'You want me to believe it?' Suddenly, he stopped in his tracks and brought down the brass-knobbed baton on the table with tremendous force, making the half-filled glass of water and the pen stand rattle.

At this point a constable quietly entered the room and whispered to the inspector.

'Sir, a couple of visitors to meet you.'

'Not today,' Thapa said irritably. 'Ask them to come some other day…unless of course it's something of earth-shattering importance.'

The irony was, unfortunately, lost on the constable.

'Sir, the elder person said it was important.'

Thapa cast him an angry look.

'They all say that.'

'Sir, I think one of them is from the monastery…an officer from Kolkata police.'

'Oh…' Thapa thought for a second. 'Did he say Avinash Roy?'

'Yes sir, I think that's the name he gave me.'

'Mr Roy coming to meet me…what could it be? Thapa looked enquiringly at Tejpal. 'All right, call him in.'

'There's another person with him, sir.'

'Okay, okay,' Thapa said impatiently. 'Call both of them in.'

The constable went out and returned with Roy and Pradyot.

'What a pleasant surprise!' exclaimed Thapa as he stretched his hand out for a handshake. 'Mr Roy…the sleuth from Calcutta. To what do I owe this rare honour?'

He clasped Roy's hand warmly.

But with the inspector you were never sure whether the enthusiasm was genuine or not.

'Now, now, you couldn't have come here just for a chit-chat with me. Or a plain cup of coffee, which, in any case, my ardali somehow manages to make quite undrinkable.'

Convent educated, Roy made a small mental correction in his estimation of the inspector.

'I hope you aren't berating your people for not being able to arrest the nun.'

'And why not?'

'Because, (a)she's not a nun and (b)she might not be a woman at all, but a swarthy, fit and extremely dangerous man.'

'What are you saying?'

Roy showed him the copy of the so-called Sister Cybil's handwriting specimen.

Thapa read the note with interest and returned it.

'So?'

'This was the nun's comment, before she left the monastery.'

'Where did you get it?'

'From Lama Tashiding.'

'Why that…' Thapa was about to foul-mouth the monk when Roy intervened.

'Let's not get into that now, Inspector. The point is, I got hold of this document and had the original sent to a graphologist friend of mine in Kolkata. And…'

'Graphologist?' Thapa scratched his head and looked quizzically at Roy.

'Isn't that someone who reads handwritings and pretends to interpret the writer's character or something like that?'

Roy gave him an ironic smile. 'Graphology is regarded as a science now. And can be quite exact. Trust me. I speak from personal experience.'

'So what does this graphologist friend of yours have to say about the handwriting?'

'I don't wish to subject you to all the technical jargon, but briefly, this is what he said: that the handwriting reveals an extremely dangerous man with pronounced murderous traits. That he can camouflage his real feelings and emotions very well; that he can exhibit an affable front while harbouring murderous thoughts inside; that he can be quite ruthless, cruel and brutal, without having any feelings of guilt whatsoever.'

'Anything else?' Thapa laughed aloud.

'Yes. Though he's not willing to put his money on it, he's reasonably sure it's a male person we are dealing with; a man with typically feminine traits which, in his case, enabled him so easily to disguise himself as a middle-aged nun.'

'My God!' Thapa slapped his forehead. 'Are you quite sure?'

The way the inspector had pronounced the word 'sure' amused Roy no end. More corrections about his education...North Point, Darjeeling perhaps?

Roy had this incorrigible habit of trying to place people.

'Or else I wouldn't have come to you,' he stated modestly. 'This is Pradyot, my assistant from Kolkata. I had him especially flown in to help me out on this case. He's staying at the Kanchenjunga Hotel. Pradyot,' he turned to his assistant,' 'will you tell the inspector what you saw this morning?'

'Yes, sir. When I was coming out of the dining hall after breakfast, I noticed a foreigner checking out of the hotel. He had a very expensive-looking trolley suitcase with him. As he was about to leave, he turned around to look at me. At that time I had paid no attention to him. A lot of foreigners come and stay at this hotel, as I learnt during my course of stay there. But, after sir told me the nun could be a man, I immediately thought of this person.'

'Any particular reasons for it?'

'Yes...the bearings of this man. There was something rather odd about him. When he turned around he seemed to look through me, as if he had X-ray eyes.'

'That's interesting!' Thapa commented.

'Also I thought it made excellent sense for him to stay close to the monastery. Because we would be looking for a nun all over Pelling. Never did we, even for once, think that she might actually be staying next door to the monastery. So, that way she was always one step ahead of us.'

'And the masterstroke was disguising himself as a woman,' added Roy.

'That put all of us on the wrong foot.'

Thapa nodded to himself.

'What did he look like?'

'Let me see...' Pradyot looked away, trying to remember.

'Initially I could only see him from behind. I would say middling height...5'6" or so. I think there was a bald patch on his crown. And then he turned around. He had pale blue eyes, an emotionless face, lifeless, ash blonde hair. What else...' Then, a quick smile appeared on his face. 'Oh yes! Now I remember...he had rather full pink lips. And he certainly didn't have a mole on his chin.'

'Brilliant!' Thapa remarked admiringly. 'I'm really surprised that you would remember so much from just one look.' He then turned to face Roy. 'I think you're very lucky to have got such an assistant.'

'The name on his passport is Antonio Vitolo. He's most probably from Italy,' Roy added. Suddenly, to his considerable discomfiture, he got a bear hug from Thapa.

'Sorry, Mr Roy...for having underestimated you.'

Sister Cybil was preparing to attend the morning prayers when Savitri bustled in and handed her a visiting card. The rest of the nuns and other inmates of the school always knocked on her door before entering. But not Savitri. For the last ten years Savitri had been her personal assistant. She tidied up her papers, washed and ironed her clothes, kept track of all her important meetings and she helped her with her medicines. In short, she had made herself quite indispensable.

'Who is it?' she asked Savitri, without taking a look at the card. She wasn't carrying her glasses, and without them she was almost blind, especially when it came to reading small print.

'A certain Inspector Setalvad, Mother. 'Has been waiting to see you for the last half an hour.'

'And why wasn't I informed about this earlier?'

Sister Cybil felt acutely embarrassed that anyone should have to wait that long just to meet her.

'You know very well, Mother,' Savitri explained to her as if she were a child. 'Because you were having your bath at that time.'

'Oh yes!' she remembered. She was having difficulty remembering things these days.

'Inspector Setalvad?' Putting on the glasses, she looked vaguely at the card. 'Have we met him before?'

'I think not,' she smiled. 'Now let me comb you hair before I pin up your cap.'

Sister Cybil had completed her eightieth birthday only the day before. It was embarrassing really, the kind of fuss the teachers made on that occasion, especially that girl Nancy, the Geography teacher. It was ridiculous that she should go all the way to the town to order a big, fat chocolate cake for her. 'As it is, I'm grossly overweight,' she'd said, 'and now you want me to end up looking like a walrus, or what?'

'What are you mumbling about, my dear?' Savitri asked, amused. 'Now turn your face this way so I can get you ready to meet this gentleman.'

Sister Cybil had come to India from Ireland when she was barely in her teens. Her father, Brian O'Keefe, an army man, had his first posting at Fort William, Calcutta, as a second lieutenant. The war was coming to an end then. And young Brian spent more time perfecting his swing at the army golf course and riding horses than conducting drills at the barracks. Within a short while, Cybil, a gangling girl with twin blond tassels swinging every which way, got her admission at the Loreto Convent school, Entally, where a certain Sister Teresa was posted then, as a teacher. It was the latter's personal example that drew the young girl to the church, though certainly not for the lack of smartly attired suitors from Fort William.

'You are ready to go now,' Savitri said, adding a little finishing touch to get the starched white cap placed just right on her thick, unruly blond head.

'Now, don't you fret, Mother, because I'm going to wheel you around.'

While the rest of the inmates addressed her as 'Sister Cybil', Savitri, for some strange reason, had always stuck to calling her 'Mother'.

Sister Cybil allowed her the levity with an indulgent smile.

The wheelchair, purchased only a few days ago, was not primarily owing to her age, though age was certainly a factor. A fortnight ago Sister Cybil had slipped in the bathroom and fractured her left leg. Savitri, of course, blamed herself for not being there, a constant tussle between the two about Sister Cybil's right to privacy, especially when it came to taking her own bath.

As it is, with age, Sister Cybil had put on weight. But now the huge plaster, stretching from the tip of her toe to her thighs, was making her look grotesquely obese. Not that she was particularly bothered by it. What really bothered her was that the injury had seriously impeded all physical movements And that was what made her despair.

Her path-breaking work amongst the tribal girls of Purulia had won her international recognition, drawing an invitation even from the Vatican. The date of invitation was less than a month away and it was going to be a race against time to get her on her feet before that. Otherwise, the crowning moment of her life might end up in nothing.

Normally, Sister Cybil would meet outsiders at the school

office. But now, lack of mobility had necessitated setting up of an improvised office, close to her living quarters.

Inspector Setalvad seemed to be a charming, old-world police officer, with a dapper little moustache, who deferentially arose from the chair as she was wheeled in. He also removed the cap from his head and deposited it on his lap.

'What's happened to you Madam…er Sister?' Setalvad was all solicitous as he looked at her leg. 'I see I've chosen a wrong moment to come here. Maybe I should drop in sometime later.'

'Don't be ridiculous, Inspector! Do sit down and stop making a mountain out of a mole hill. I'm perfectly all right and mobile… thanks to my lucky mascot here.' She gave Savitri an affectionate pat on her shoulder. 'Now, first let me tender my sincere apologies, Inspector, for keeping you waiting so long. The fact is I wasn't quite aware that you would be coming to meet me. So, what is it that you've come about…Inspector?'

The inspector gently coughed, pointedly looking in the direction of Savitri.

'Sister Cybil…if we could…er,' he darted another uncomfortable look at Savitri. 'If we could have a little more privacy.'

'What rubbish!' she shot a glance at Savitri and laughed aloud. 'There are no secrets between us. She knows all that I know about this institution, and at times, things that even I don't.'

Setalvad demurred, but still held his ground.

'Sister Cybil, it's on your own account that I wish to talk to you in private.'

The seriousness in his voice made her roll up her eyes in mock horror and give in.

'Okay, so be it, Savitri…off you go. Otherwise we will never get to the bottom of the dark little secret behind the inspector's visit.'

Savitri, though, seemed to take no offence at his insistence on privacy.

'Do give me a call when it's all over,' she indicated the brass bell on the table as she left, closing the door gently behind her.

'Yes…' Sister Cybil said, her tongue firmly in cheek. 'You have your desired privacy now.'

Inspector Setalvad took his time before speaking.

'It's about Miriam's death in Pelling. Miriam de Gonzales… she died an unnatural death, I'm afraid. Perhaps a murder.'

Sister Cybil seemed not to comprehend.

'What are you saying, Inspector? I don't really follow you.'

'I understand,' Setalvad said softly. 'It's difficult for you to accept this. Apparently you used to be awfully fond of her.'

'Miriam is in Pelling. She's expected to be back here by the end of the month,' she said stubbornly.

'Sister Cybil…' This time he spoke a little louder. 'I'm afraid that's not going to be so now. Miriam's dead. Perhaps it's murder. That's why I've come here to investigate about her.'

'Now hang on a sec,' she had a troubled look on her face. 'There was an email letter a couple of days ago, from one Mr Roy…I think.'

'What was it about, do you remember?'

'Let me see now…I think he wanted to know if I had visited Pelling of late and had sent a sample of handwriting, to verify if it was mine.'

A pause.

'Me, in my present condition, travelling to Pelling? Quite amusing really.' She said with a sad smile. 'If Miriam's dead then why didn't this gentleman inform me at that time?'

'Perhaps he didn't want to hurt your feelings…I can't really say.'

She looked helplessly around for support.

'Do you want me to call the attendant, Sister?'

'Yes please. Her name's Savitri.'

Inspector Setalvad got up from his chair and pressed the bell on the table.

Savitri appeared in the room in no time.

'Your meeting's over so soon?' she said in an amused tone. But one look at her and the smile vanished from her face.

'What is it, Mother?'

'Savitri, come here quick. The gentleman here says Miriam's dead. Murdered. Tell him that's impossible. She's to be ordained here next month.'

Savitri looked alternately at Sister Cybil and Inspector Setalvad in mute horror.

'Inspector, tell me it's all lies…you just made it up.'

The inspector gently shook his head.

'I'm afraid it's true. You can call up the monastery in Pelling and verify.

The two women clung to each other and cried silently.

'There's more bad news. Not only was Miriam murdered in Pelling, we have reasons to suspect that the seeds of the murder were planted out here, in Coorg.'

'What are you saying?' Sister Cybil's voice sounded shrill and high pitched. 'Have you taken leave of your senses, Inspector?'

'What I've stated is true. And the sooner you accept it, the better for all of us.'

'But inspector, you are implicating us. That we are involved in the murder. That is a perfectly despicable thing to say.'

Her voice wasn't loud anymore. But it was clear that she was digging her heels in, spoiling for a fight.

'Madam…you heard me wrong. I didn't implicate you in the

murder, or this institution. I only said we have reasons to suspect that something happened out here in Coorg which finally led to her murder in Pelling.

Suddenly, as Sister Cybil recalled something from the past, it sent a chill down her spine.

'Okay…I'm ready.' She sniffed hard, causing her nose to turn red. 'Shoot.'

Setalvad raised his left hand in a pacifying gesture.

'This is not war, ma'am. I'm sure you would be as interested in finding out who killed Miriam as anybody else. Perhaps even more, because she was so dear to all of you.'

Sister Cybil seemed somewhat mollified by this gesture.

'Let me recount what happened at Pelling. We discussed the murder with the police officers working on the case on Skype only last night. Miriam was killed three nights ago, smothered to death with a pillow on her bed. That day she had received a visitor in the afternoon, a nun by the name of Sister Cybil.'

Setalvad waited for some reaction from her. But there was none.

'We know she was a fake.'

The two women exchanged glances, but didn't say anything.

'We have reasons to believe that she not only faked her identity, but also her sex.'

'What do you mean?' Sister Cybil couldn't help asking.

'That, in fact, he was a man, disguised as a woman.'

'That's impossible! Miriam would never do such a thing. Allow a man to sleep with her knowingly.'

'Yes, you're so right,' he stated thoughtfully. 'That's the million dollar question. Why would she allow a man, disguised as a woman, to sleep with her knowingly?'

A long pause.

'Unless of course she knew him/her beforehand?'

The women remained silent, not commenting.

'Do you know if she had a boyfriend?'

'Ridiculous question.'

'But needs to be answered all the same.'

'No, she didn't.' She looked at Savitri. 'Did she have a boyfriend, you think?'

Savitri vehemently shook her head.

'Then who was this person?'

Again silence from Sister Cybil and Savitri.

'According to the monks in Pelling, this was the only time she had received a visitor in the last five years.'

Setalvad stared long and hard at Sister Cybil.

'It stands to reason, then, that the only place where he could've made contact with her was here, in Coorg.'

Another long pause.

'Any comments?'

She shook her head.

'You're forcing me to ask the question.' His jaw muscles hardened imperceptively. 'No problem...did Miriam receive any male visitor, a male visitor of foreign origin, a white Caucasian, before she left for Pelling this time?'

She had a sinking feeling in the pit of her stomach. She had been dreading this question for more than a month now. From the very day this foreigner, with his very expensive shoes, had visited the school and asked for a private meeting with Miriam. If truth be told, she hadn't been a part of that meeting. She had no idea as to what had transpired between the two of them. And, after that meeting was over and the gentleman had left, she hadn't asked Miriam anything. But, she had noticed, because it was fairly easy to read Miriam's face, that she was acutely unhappy about the whole thing. As if she had been asked to do something that was contrary to her nature.

'Yes or no?' Setalvad looked intensely at Sister Cybil.

'She may have,' she said at last.

Any trace of a smile smile had gone from his face.

'I need a definitive answer…yes or no?'

Sister Cybil had never lied in her whole life before, at least not knowingly. And now, her character was being severely tested.

'Yes.'

'Do you have his card?'

'He didn't give me any.'

'Do you remember his name, at least?'

'Antonio Vitolo, I think.'

A faint smile appeared on Setalvad's face. The inspector from Pelling had mentioned the same name to him on Skype.

'Hmm…' Setalvad scratched his chin thoughtfully.

'Antonio Vitolo! You better open up Sister…tell me everything you know about him. Who's he…where did he come from…who sent him…and why…everything.'

Sister Cybil was thrown into a huge moral dilemma. How much was she going to tell him? Would he believe her if she disclosed whatever she knew? As it is, she knew so precious little.

'I'm waiting to hear from you, Sister.'

She cleared her throat, looked once at Savitri, then started speaking.

'I can't tell you the exact date…but last month I suddenly received an international phone call. I really don't know where it came from. But it changed hands several times before the final call came through.'

'Meaning?'

'Meaning…several people spoke on the line, before the final caller did.'

'Who was the last speaker?'

'Don't know.'

'What do you mean you don't know?'

'The second last voice simply said, "Please wait…the Archbishop would like to speak with you," that's all.'

She resumed after a period of silence.

'I was so overawed by the occasion that it never occurred to me to find out who the final caller was.'

'So, you know him simply as the Archbishop?'

She nodded.

'Do you use a cell phone?'

'Yes, I do.'

'Did the call come through on your cell phone?'

'Unfortunately not. Then I could've perhaps given you the caller's number.'

Setalvad simply nodded a couple of times.

'Tell me everything that you remember of that conversation.'

'Well…it was brief and courteous. The gentleman first asked me about how our school was functioning. So, I told him it was running fine. We had no major problems. Then he asked me if I was prepared to do something good for the church. So, I said yes, of course! You can certainly count on me, your holiness. This seemed to please him. Then he asked me if we had a girl called Miriam teaching in our school. I said yes. Then he gently enquired about Miriam, if she was religious, pious and obedient—all that.'

'And what did you say to that?'

'I said, of course, she's one of the best we have and that she was shortly going to join our order. So, he asked me if she could be relied upon to do something good for the church, for the cause of Christianity. And I said, I think she could.'

'And then?'

'Only then did this man say that he would like to meet Miriam and talk to her. And that the entire thing should remain a secret between the two of us. That the lesser the number of people who knew about it, the better.'

'I see...that was all? You never asked him why it should remain a secret.'

'No, I was too scared to.'

Setalvad stroked his chin thoughtfully. 'Now describe this man to me.'

'The man who came here...Antonio?'

'Yes, who else could we be talking about?'

'Antonio Vitolo...' Sister Cybil thought for a while. 'He was expensively dressed. One would've thought that he was from the World Bank or UNO—the kind of look he had. He was well-mannered. But rather withdrawn and secretive. Spoke very little.'

'Secretive...how did you figure that out?'

'Well, at the end of the meeting I knew just nothing about him. I don't think he even formally introduced himself. And... that's about all I suppose.'

'I think you were about to say something after 'and', but stopped short.'

'Something that I wasn't quite sure of, so I thought why talk about it.'

'You can tell me without hesitation, even if you aren't sure. I would understand.'

'Somehow...how do I describe it, somehow he made you feel uncomfortable...something about his eyes. He seldom blinked. And yes, he had pink nails and pink lips. Somewhat effeminate.'

'Anything else?'

'No…nothing else seems to come to my mind just now.'

Setalvad smiled. 'Well, if you do remember anything later, just call me up at this number.'

He extended his card to Sister Cybil who, in turn, passed it on to Savitri.

'There, it will be in safe hands now. Somehow I always manage to misplace these things.' She seemed to be enormously relieved that the ordeal was over now. The gentleman was quite well-mannered really. But then, you never enjoy being interrogated by the police.

The inspector stood up and thanked her sincerely for patiently answering all his questions and assured her that he had no intentions of intimidating her.

'Oh! One last thing…if it's any consolation to you, Miriam wasn't violated by this man.'

Once inside the car, the inspector took his cell phone out of the pocket and started playing it back. It seemed that he had recorded the entire conversation with the nun surreptitiously. After satisfying himself that the recording was all right, he dialled a particular number and played back the entire stuff. When it was over, there was a chorus of voices from the other end, thanking him profusely. It seemed that the recipient of the call had put it on microphone so that others could also listen in.

'Excellent work, Inspector Setalvad. As far as Antonio Vitolo is concerned, your description of him quite matches with our impression, whatever we've been able to gather about him. But, what do you think of the Sister? Was she speaking the truth?'

'I think so,' came the amused reply. 'She seems to be the kind of god-fearing person to whom lying is a cardinal sin.'

When Antonio Vitolo came out of the toilet he looked a different man. The ice-blue eyes had been replaced by a shade of hazel brown. The clean-shaven corporate look was gone. Instead, what he had was a thick, droopy, Pancho Gonzales moustache that gave him a definite South American look, someone from Mexico or Colombia perhaps.

The changes were nothing pronounced. Just a little bit of thickening of the eyebrows, putting on a baseball cap the other way round, a little cleft on the chin. But all these toted up, gave him a significantly different look.

The first thing that he did after coming out of the loo was to exchange his fancy, unbreakable fiberglass trolley suitcase with a khaki, canvas backpack. A pair of worn-out jeans and used, red canvas casual shoes completed the transformation.

The great thing about Antonio was his supreme confidence in himself. He was reasonably sure no one would be able to trace him back to his former Mrs Doubtfire avatar.

Antonio prided on never repeating himself. But, this time he thought he needn't take so much care. He used the same gents toilet in the town's only shopping mall that he had used three days ago, to emerge as Mrs Doubtfire. The Doubtfire thing had been a little tricky, because it involved his coming out of a gents toilet as a woman. But nothing untoward had happened in that instance. Had a man stepped into the toilet just then, he would've had some ready answer like, 'Sorry my dear, but the lady's toilet is simply unusable.'

The warm sun felt good on his pale skin. He took out a pack of long thin cigars and lit one. He took a deep drag and slowly exhaled through his half-open, girlishly pouted mouth and enjoyed the aroma of the Dutch tobacco. He felt no urge to run. Only fools run after the act. You relax. You just keep your eyes and ears open to make sure no one's following you. That's all.

He felt strangely at peace with himself after the double murder. No conscience pricks, no regrets. That woman had it coming for her. Once you agreed with Antonio on something there's no way you could renege on it. She had failed to play the part that she had been assigned to. That's why she had to pay the price. As for the young monk, Tenzing, he felt elated at having slit his throat, knowing very well that the woman had the hots for him. If you want to be a nun, you have to remain chaste. It's as simple as that. Too bad that Tenzing had been an accomplice.

His only regret in the whole affair was that he had not been able to lay hands on the manuscript. But he wouldn't deem it a failure on his part. It was more the result of faulty planning, based on unreliable information. Perhaps the manuscript hadn't been brought there at all. In which case one would have to track it back to the Hemis monastery in Ladakh. People often spread misinformation intentionally to keep mercenaries and treasure hunters at bay. Talking of mercenaries, he didn't consider himself to be one. He liked to be regarded as an emissary of the church, if not God himself.

He leisurely walked across to a roadside shanty tea stall, sat on a rickety chair and asked for a masala chai and desi biscuits. He really loved the crumbly, fluffiness of the local cookies. As he sat sipping chai from an earthen cup, he idly watched a police Jeep leaving the township and speeding towards Dengziang monastery. He felt amused and relaxed. Let them go and investigate to their heart's content. What did he care?

In the unlikely scenario of the local police catching up with his real identity, he knew the first thing they would try and do would be to post lookouts for him at airports, railway stations and inter-state bus terminuses. They would mount vigil at all road checkpoints to prevent his escape. Pelling and the neighbouring townships were not connected by rail or air. So, they would expect him to travel to Siliguri first and then plan his escape, for Siliguri presented one with multiple escape options.

He took out a large folded map of Sikkim from his rucksack and spread it across the table, careful not to spill tea on it. He first located Pelling on the map and drew a small circle around the name with a red marker. So, that's where he was right now.

Now, to the planning of his escape route. The easiest way to get caught by the police would be to hire a private cab and travel down to Siliguri by road. Travelling by bus or a pool taxi was better. But not good enough. If the police were serious about him, they would put up metal barriers across roads, check each and every passing vehicle, making all passengers step out in the open. He briefly thought about being a pillion rider to a local biker. Hippies on shoestring budgets often favour that kind of ride. But no. That too, was out. He had to look at it from a totally different angle. An escape route that the police wouldn't even think of. He stared at the map for a long time. Then a girlish smile appeared on his full lips.

Roy was still at the police station when word came through that someone had found a large plastic bag hidden in a bush, somewhere between the monastery and the Kanchenjunga Hotel. Inside the bag was a full-length black cloak, a ginger coloured wig such as worn by women, and what was even more interesting, a padded pair of bras, filled with rubber foam. Sensing something wrong, the fellow had come straight to the police station to report it. As a matter of fact, this man was right now waiting outside the room.

'Well, what are we waiting for? Call him in.'

To Roy he said in an amused tone, 'The nun's story, wrapped in a plastic bag!'

Thapa's guess was hundred per cent correct. The plastic bag did contain all that was reported to them.

Rummaging through the pockets of the black cassock, Roy came up with a small container as was used to store jewellery. He opened the lid and looked inside. There it was, a large jelly-like substance almost quivering alive, the nun's pink mole.

Everyone who looked at it was taken aback.

'Sir,' the man who had found the bag beseeched, 'I bring you valuables. Some baksheesh, please.'

The man went away happily, as Thapa pressed a 500-rupee note into his hands.

'I hope now there is no doubt that our Sister Cybil and Antonio Vitolo are not different persons, but one,' Roy stated.

Thapa nodded his head. 'So it would seem.'

Roy got up from his seat as did Pradyot. 'I'll take your leave then. I hope I've been of some help at least'.

'How many days more are you here?' Thapa asked, as they were about to leave.

'A few days more, till I wrap up my private business here.'

'I was wondering…provided you have the time and inclination of course, if you would like to be a part of our team…to hunt this man out.'

From Pelling to the border of Nepal, Antonio figured, couldn't be more than 60–70 kilometres as the crow flies. He chose this route after a lot of thought and consideration. First and foremost, nobody in his senses would ever think of such an outlandish route of exit from the country, for he had to exit from India, and as quickly as possible. If the police were ever to latch on to his real identity the first thing they would do would be to inform all airports to be on the lookout for a certain Antonio Vitolo and impound his passport as soon as they saw it. Ditto for all land routes.

For a while he had even considered crossing over to Bangladesh. His map showed it could easily be done once he was in North Bengal. But that, he learnt, might entail travelling by road, which he was determined to avoid.

So, all things said and done, Nepal was his safest bet. He could even pinpoint the place on the other side of the border, a place called Tumling Ter, in Nepal. It couldn't be much more than a village. From there it would be fairly easy to reach Biratnagar, a comparatively large border town with a flourishing inter-state trade. The India-Nepal border was porous all along. So, crossing over illegally shouldn't pose any problems for him. Once there, he could easily melt into the thousands and thousands of tourists who throng Nepal every day.

There was no motorable road connecting the two places. It was doubtful if there would even be a fair weather path through the dense jungle, once he passed through the cluster of villages nearby. After that it was good riddance to civilization. He would've vanished into the forest without a trace. The more remote and difficult the route, he reasoned, the better it was for him.

Having made his decision, he neatly folded the map before putting it back into the rucksack. He finished the chai in one large gulp and threw the earthen cup expertly into the bin a good ten feet away. He then strolled across to the Government Tourism Information Centre nearby to enquire about popular trekking routes emanating from Pelling. The young lady behind the counter was quite helpful and suggested Yuksom to him. Yuksom, she said, had a clearly defined trekking route, with well-maintained shacks for overnight halts, and was a popular destination with foreign tourists. As a matter of fact, a group of six tourists had come this morning to their centre for information on the Yuksom route and, if he wanted, he could contact them at a nearby hotel.'

'When are they leaving?' Antonio asked.

'Tomorrow,' she said.

He nodded a couple of times.

'And if I wish to trek somewhere else?'

The lady took out a folder containing all the trekking routes in Sikkim. 'Here,' she extended the folder across the counter.

'This is where we are, in Pelling.' She came forward to point it out on the map. In doing so, her hair brushed against his face.

'I'm sorry,' she pulled back a little.

'It's all right.' He found her physical proximity rather enjoyable.

'If you don't wish to go to Yuksom, you could come down to a village named Dentam. And then, you turn left and come to a place called Bermoik. But, after that it's a long and tortuous route to Chewa Bhanjyang. So I won't advocate it. It would be better if you took the route to Darap, then turn left to Nambu. From there you go to Chonri, Yambong and, finally, to Dafeybhir.'

'Dafeybhir, going by this map, is near the Nepal border?'

'You're right, it is.'

'Any other route that you would like to suggest?'

'Well let's see…you could go to Khechuperi Lakes by road. And from there you could go past Yuksom to Psoka and then to Phedong and finally to Kokchurong. But that's a reasonably long route and you might like to take a sherpa with you to carry your stuff.'

The gentleman, who hadn't as yet introduced himself by name, looked affluent enough to afford a sherpa for the trip.

'A sherpa?'

'Oh! A porter who specializes in carrying things for you on mountain trips.'

The man stared at the map for a long time and nodded to himself.

'Yeah,' he said, making up his mind. 'I'll either go to Yuksom or Kokchurong. First thing tomorrow morning.'

'You've got your own trekking stuff? Otherwise you can hire them from a local shop here.'

'Oh! That's great. I think I'll hire the kit. Where is this shop?'

'Come, I'll show you.' She drew him close to her and pointed out. 'You see that shopping mall? It's just beyond that. A place called Trekker's Hut.'

'Oh! Thanks so much for taking all the trouble. Can I have this folder please?'

'But of course! It's meant for you.'

As she gave him the folder, their hands touched.

'Thank you so much,' he said and left.

The girl at the Centre seemed very eager to please him, he thought. He turned back to find her still smiling and waving at him. Just for a brief moment he was tempted to take her to bed and make prolonged love to her, till she cried out in ecstasy. But he quickly banished all such thoughts from his mind. Never mix business with pleasure.

He weighed in his mind as to what to do. The last thing that he wanted was to travel with a bunch of boisterous youngsters, asking him silly questions like where he was from and which place he was headed for. The whole thing had to be done in secrecy. He decided then and there that he would leave Pelling that afternoon itself, alone. He knew now what his final plans were. And he was going to keep them close to his chest. Leave, he smiled to himself. But leave no footprints behind.

Things had started happening fast with the infusion of Roy and Pradyot in the team. 'The first thing that we need to do is discard the police Jeep and van,' he had said. 'No need to advertise to our Antonio that we are after him. The same goes for your uniforms. Change into civvies so that he does not recognize us as police.'

Accordingly, they had all piled into Inspector Thapa's private car. But not before they had stripped it of all police identities. So that now it looked like any other car in Pelling, only a little shinier and better maintained, perhaps.

They had first paid a visit to Kanchenjunga Hotel, talked to the receptionist to find out whatever they could about Antonio. Upon enquiring they found that the foreigner's hotel booking had been made locally, by a lady. This was highly revealing. Could it be then that Antonio's booking had been made beforehand by Miriam? And that was when Pradyot had seen her for the first time as she was heading for the hotel? They also found out which private cab had picked up the foreigner from the hotel that morning. They had then tagged the driver of that cab and found out where exactly he had dropped his passenger off in the township.

'What are you staring at?' Thapa asked Roy. They were standing where the cab driver had said he had dropped off the foreigner. In front of them was the busy marketplace, and the only shopping mall in Pelling.

'This shopping mall…what's it called?'

'Big Bazaar, I think.'

'It's fairly new by the look of it.'

'Yeah…opened only last year. Why?'

'Might have been used as a changing room by Antonio.'

'Changing room…what do you mean?' Thapa couldn't help asking.

'See,' Roy reasoned, 'if we do a quick reconstruct of the last few days with reference to Antonio, what do we find?'

'You tell me.' Thapa muttered, still not getting the drift of Roy's thinking.

'Let's go back three days—Antonio checks into Kanchenjunga Hotel late in the morning, as Antonio. Right?'

'Yes, I'll go along with that. Because I looked into the hotel's register book. Time of entry…11.30 a.m.'

'Good. He's probably come straight from Bagdogra airport. We can easily check that out by consulting the flight manifest of all the planes that landed at Bagdogra that particular morning. That would also account for where he came from.'

'You want me to do that now?'

'Yes, you may. But right now it wouldn't make any difference to our line of thinking. The important thing is that the same afternoon Antonio makes an appearance at Dengziang, as Sister Cybil.'

Thapa agreed.

'The question is where did he change into Sister Cybil? Not at the hotel, at least. That would immediately arouse suspicion. Where did this nun suddenly appear from, they would wonder.'

'At a bush nearby?' Thapa suggested. 'Remember, our ragpicker guy found the plastic bag hidden behind a bush very close to our scene of action. So, let's say he leaves the hotel as Antonio, carrying the cassock and other things in a bag. On the way he finds the bush and hides behind it. When he comes out a little later, it's as Sister Cybil. How about that?'

'Excellent thinking...but the only problem with that is Sister Cybil didn't arrive at the monastery on foot. She came in a red Maruti van, driven by this rockstar driver, whatever his name is...'

'Mad Max.'

'Yes, Mad Max. And this chap says he picked her up from the market, right in front of the shopping mall. So, chances are that our man went to the town market as Antonio, found a convenient place where he could change into the nun's garb and then emerged as Sister Cybil.'

'Yah, that makes sense.'

'So, we come back to the original question. Where did he change? We know it has to be in the town.'

Thapa pondered for a while, then shrugged undecidedly.

'The answer probably lies inside,' Roy said, indicating the shopping mall in front. 'Let's go and find out.'

It was a two-storied complex, displaying the usual stuff; readymade clothing, shoes, junk jewellery, toiletries and cosmetic products, soft toys, a coffee shop. They made a quick recce of shops on both floors, to figure out where Antonio might have changed his identity. But found none. Finally, on their way out, they stopped in front of the toilet. It had two sections—gents and ladies. The gents toilet was clean and functional—standing urinals on one side and a washing area with three basins in a row and a large mirror in front. Roy looked at Thapa through the mirror.

'I think he changed here.'

'What makes you think so?'

Roy walked to the door and locked it from inside.

'You see...now he has total privacy. He quickly changes into Sister Cybil. Fixing the padded bras and the mole need much more time and attention. More importantly, he needs a mirror in front and ample light, to make sure that the mole sits perfectly on his face. That done, she steps out of the mall and hails the red Maruti van and reaches Dengziang Monastery.'

Thapa thought quietly for a while and nodded. 'Possible.'

As they came out, Thapa asked, 'If you were Antonio, how would you plan your escape?'

Roy stood at the entrance of the mall, watching people entering and leaving.

'The first thing that I would do would be to change my identity again. No more as Mrs Doubtfire.'

'Ha ha!' Thapa laughed aloud. 'That's what I was thinking of. In which movie had I seen a man change into a buxom woman?'

Hands stroking his chin, Roy kept looking around.

'I would change into someone who jells with the surrounds.'

He idly watched a couple of foreigners pass by, rucksacks on their back.

'Yeah, why not a trekker?' He said at length. 'Pelling has always been a popular destination for trekkers.'

The Tourism Information Centre was only a stone's throw away. They walked across and asked for information on popular trekking routes starting out of Pelling. The young lady behind the counter took a good look at them and smiled.

'It's great to be young at heart, sir. After all, age is just a number, isn't it?'

Roy and Thapa looked at each other, then smiled back to her.

'Thank you for the compliment.'

She came out with a folder that provided details of trekking routes from Pelling.

'The best trekking route, of course, is the journey to Yuksom. Did you know it used to be the earliest capital of Sikkim? All that is gone now, though. Nothing remains of the original royal palace.'

'I see, Roy said. 'The Yuksom route…it's quite popular with

the foreign tourists, isn't it?'

'Oh yes!' she beamed. 'During the season we get enquiries from them every day.'

'By any chance did you get any such enquiries today? Roy asked casually.

'As a matter of fact, we did.' Her eyes lit up as she spoke. 'There was this foreigner who came in just a couple of hours ago. And I put him on to six other tourists who are planning to go to Yuksom first thing tomorrow.'

'Great! We'll surely like to meet up with these gentlemen. 'Much better if we travel with them. We're sort of first-timers, you see. Would you care to describe the gentleman who came here alone?'

The lady looked a little surprised at them. 'But…'

'Plain curiosity. I had happened to meet a foreigner who talked about going to Yuksom a few days ago. Just wondering if he is the same guy.'

Thus reassured, the lady opened up to them quite willingly.

'Let me see… he didn't sound like an Englishman; spoke with a definite accent. Sported a drooping moustache, kind of Spanish or Mexican. A baseball cap, worn the other way round, like the kids of today.'

'Was he young, then?'

'I won't say that. He looked fortyish to me. He had a khaki canvas rucksack on his back. He seemed to be quite nice though… nice smile.'

Thapa looked a little perplexed.

'He doesn't seem to be our man,' he said in a low voice.

'On the contrary, this could very well be his new identity,' Roy whispered back.

'What colour eyes did he have? Do you remember if it was ice blue?'

'No, not blue,' she tried to remember. 'More light brown like.'

'What about his height, middling?'

'Yes... I'd say shorter than you.' She looked at Roy, giving him a once-over.

'What were his clothes like?'

'I think he wore faded blue jeans and a windcheater.'

'Exactly what conversation did this man have with you?'

'But why are you asking so many questions about him?' she asked, a little alarmed.

Thapa and Roy looked at each other before the former spoke.

'You see, madam, we didn't wish to scare you off. But since you ask I might as well tell you. I am Inspector Thapa, Chief of Police in Pelling.' He produced his ID from his pocket and showed it to her. 'This man is a bit of a crook; he borrowed money from my friend,' he said, indicating Roy. 'And didn't pay back. So, we're looking for him.'

'Is that so?' her eyes widened in surprise. 'He looked a decent sort of guy, though.'

'Yup,' Thapa nodded gravely. 'Looks can be deceptive. I hope you don't mind answering our questions now.'

'No no, anything at all to help the police.'

'What questions did he ask?' This time it was Roy. 'Anything to do with trekking?'

'How did you know that?' she looked quite surprised. 'As a matter of fact, he did. He asked about the popular trekking routes from Pelling. So, I told him about Yuksom and then... I also told him about Dafeybhir.'

'This Dafeybhir... where exactly is it? Please point it out to us on the map.'

She showed it. They exchanged significant glances and stared at the map.

'It's on the Nepal border all right. What else did he say?'

'He said he would be leaving first thing tomorrow, either for Yuksom, or Kokchurong.'

'Kokchurong?'

She indicated it to them on the map. A thin smile appeared on Roy's face.

'Both of them red herrings,' he said under his breath. 'What else?'

'I...I told him where he could get trekking kits on hire.'

'You did?'

'Yes, a place called Trekker's Hut. It's...'

'I know where it is.' Thapa said.

'Well, thanks so much...you've been of great help,' Roy shook hands with her warmly. 'Now if you kindly tell me where these foreigners are staying.'

The lady jotted down the name of the hotel on a piece of paper and gave it to him. Roy and Thapa thanked her again and left the information centre.

'I think we've got our man now,' Roy said, as they walked back towards the car.

'Are you sure?'

'You're never sure,' Roy shrugged. 'But at least it's something to work on. And, while we are at it, you might like to brief your men to spread out with the latest description of Antonio and find out if any of the shopkeepers had any dealings with him this afternoon. Ask them to especially enquire inside the mall since we know he's been there. And the place called Trekker's Hut.'

Thapa went back to the car and talked to his men, Pradyot included. When he came back, Roy gave him the lady's handwritten note.

'Do you know this place?'

Thapa nodded his head.

But when they went over to the hotel and met the six tourists, they said no one had as yet contacted them for the Yuksom trip.

'That's strange. What do we do now?'

Roy pulled at his chin, thinking. 'I think he's left one red herring after another behind him, to put us off the scent…Yuksom, Kokchurong, everything. And if he's said he's leaving first thing in the morning, then in all likelihood he's leaving or has already left today.'

'What makes you so sure?'

'Can we take a walk back, if you don't mind? I think better that way.'

It was a strange sight, the two lonely figures in the gathering gloom, walking down an empty road. And a big car, its lights dimmed, crawling after them.

'You see…our Antonio isn't a trekker. He is only posing as one. Yuksom can never be his destination; getting out of this country is. So, think of where he is likely to go. I think, his actual destination is Nepal. The girl at the centre mentioned Dafeybhir. That's where he's headed for.'

Suddenly he was galvanized into action.

'Let's go back. We have no time to lose.'

They took the car to drive back to the shopping mall and asked everyone to join them. They had to go back to the police station immediately. Pradyot and Tejpal, who had in the meantime worked out a good equation between themselves, had something interesting to report. Antonio had apparently exchanged the expensive fiberglass trolley suitcase for a canvas rucksack in one of the shops in the mall. The jacket too had been exchanged for a synthetic windcheater. And yes, this guy had, indeed, gone to Trekker's Hut and hired a shoulder holdall that could accommodate a portable, lightweight tent.

'Good, the hunt is on now.'

Thapa's sneezing bouts had stopped altogether.

In winter the sun dips behind the hills and you think suddenly someone's poured, jet black ink on earth. It gets dark that fast.

Antonio had been walking steadily for the past one hour, avoiding the main road and its sporadic traffic. It was a fairly easy thing to do. In the winding hilly roads you could hear an approaching car long before you actually saw it. First there's a faint buzz, like that of a drone. Then the sound magnifies, echoing and re-echoing, against the hills, till you think a huge monster is upon you. Then, suddenly, at the turn of the road, you spot twin orbs of light getting bigger and bigger. And before you've even realized, it's rushed past you, plunging everything into total darkness.

He had left Pelling in the afternoon itself. Something, call it sixth sense, had prompted him to change his mind and leave the town quickly. Initially, he had thought of lying low for a while in Pelling itself, under disguise, and wait for the police heat to die. They would mount a desperate manhunt for him, in this case a womanhunt...poor fools at all exit points—New Jalpaiguri, Bagdogra airport, at all road intersections. Failing to find her, they would think she had somehow managed to give them the slip and left the country. He knew it happened everywhere in the world. If you couldn't make headway in a murder case within the first week, it inevitably got pushed to the backburner. Unless, of course, a VIP was involved. Miriam and Tenzing certainly didn't fall into that category. So, he knew he was reasonably safe there.

But his mind had been restless since morning. Something,

some little incident, maybe just a stray glance from a passer-by in the streets, was bugging him. Was it that tall wiry looking man that he had chanced upon as he was checking out of the hotel? Their eyes had met only for a brief second. But even that was long enough for him. Those eyes were searching, measuring you up all the time. The eyes of a cop? Or an army man? Only they had those kind of eyes. And professional killers, of course.

Or was it the lack of police activity at the ground level? Barring that one time around midday, when he had noticed a police Jeep and van heading towards Dengziang Monastery, there had been hardly any police movement at all. But, shouldn't there have been so? Two murders, taking place in quick succession, in a small sleepy town like Pelling should have sent the local police into frenetic activity. But he had noticed none. That, too, had raised his hackles. And he had survived all this while because he was possessed of very fine hackles, indeed.

So he had left. He had left in the afternoon itself. The idea was to carry on walking along the road from Pelling to Darap. At Darap there would be a road-intersection, one taking you to Yuksom, the other, to Nambu. He had at one point even debated taking a car up to Darap that would've saved him a lot of time. But, he had acted against it. Instinct told him to have as few witnesses as possible of his departure.

At Darap he avoided the route to Yuksom and took the road left, to Nambu. Once he reached Nambu, he would be on his own. There was no motorable road beyond this point.

Did that worry him? Not really. He knew there was a well-defined trekking route from Nambu that took you, via Chonri and Yambong, to Dafeybhir.

Once you reached Dafeybhir you were a free bird. From there you could happily cross over to Nepal.

At Nambu, before moving away from the road, he took a short break. There was a tea stall nearby. He sat there sipping the sweet, strong tea. He missed the locally made cookies that he had liked so much at Pelling. After paying for his tea he left the road. He took out the powerful LED torch that he had brought with him. The trekking route was clearly visible, even in the dark. There was nothing to worry about, he told himself.

A little before reaching Chonri he veered away from the marked route. Chonri, he knew, had a campsite. And he didn't want himself to be seen. He was sure that he had turned left from the trekking route. But after only five minutes, he hit a dense jungle. That was all right. The jungle would give him perfect cover. He had actually looked forward to it. But, after travelling for half an hour, he realized he might have lost his way. He had turned right to come back to the trekking trail, but couldn't find it. He spent another half an hour walking towards what he thought was the right direction. But the trekking trail remained elusive.

How could that be? He stopped dead in his tracks. It was 8 p.m. now by his watch. He didn't want to spend the rest of the night trying to find the trail and unnecessarily tire himself out. Better to pitch the tent here for the night. And return to the trail after daybreak. But as he was hammering in the pegs, he seemed to hear strange sounds around him. Was something slithering away over the dry leaves? Was this area infested with snakes? He had no idea. He unsheathed the Swiss knife from the rucksack and waited. But nothing happened. No wild animal made an attack. He wasn't sure if pitching the tent here, in the middle of the jungle, was such a good idea. So he packed up the tent and started walking. There had to be a village somewhere nearby. India was packed with villages. So, he walked steadily for a little while, looking for a light, a lamp, anything.

A little later he glimpsed a faint light to his left. But, it seemed to be mobile. So, it couldn't be a hutment. Must be someone like him, moving through the night. He started walking in the direction of the light. If he could somehow meet up with a local guy, he could at least find out exactly where he was and get direction from him on the location of the trekking route. But, when he was nearing the source of the light something unexpected happened. As he lit the torch and focused it on the person, the latter took fright and ran for his life. After a while Antonio gave up the chase. It was no good. He stood bent forward, holding on to his knees, trying to regain his breath. His plan of leaving Pelling in the afternoon wasn't panning out so well. It might have been better for him if he had left the morning next. Maybe it would've been a better idea to have hired a Sherpa for the trip as the girl from the information centre had suggested. At least he wouldn't have lost his way like this.

Anyway, no use blaming himself now. He had trusted his instincts and left that afternoon. And it were his instincts that had been his saviour in the past. He sat down under a tree, fixed the torch in such a position as to throw light upwards, so that the branches and the leaves acted as an umbrella and lit up the place. He hunted for some dry twigs and made a small fire to heat a readymade packet of noodles. As he ate it with his finger, it hadn't occurred to him to buy a fork in Pelling, he realized he had been ravenously hungry.

What to do next, he tried to figure out. By sheer providence help came his way. He heard some footsteps and turned around to find a man with a small boy with him. He said 'namaste' and smiled. The man, with a thin blanket around him, reciprocated.

At least these two hadn't run away from him.

'I want shelter for the night.' Without wasting time he brought out three hundred rupee notes from the wallet and offered it to him. Should be incentive enough for the poor villager to help him. But it wasn't clear if the man understood. He kept looking at the notes in his hand and at his face.

'*Kyon… kya chahte ho?*'

Antonio folded his hands, pretending it was a pillow and put his head sidewise on them. He then closed his eyes.

'I want a place to sleep for the night.'

The villager looked at him, then at his own boy. The boy suddenly giggled, making the man laugh out too. Antonio smiled back.

'*Humro saath ao.*' The man motioned him to get up.

Antonio felt immensely relieved. He had been understood.

It was Pierre's last night in Pelling. His shooting had been over the day before. The crew members had all left with their equipment. The monastery wore a deserted look. So did the Kanchenjunga Hotel.

He went up to Lama Phunsok's quarters to bid him goodbye, thanked him for all the help, then came back to the guesthouse. He was somewhat surprised to find Roy back. The last few days he had hardly seen him at the monastery.

'So you finally remembered us.'

Roy just smiled in response.

'I hear you are leaving.'

'Yeah,' he nodded a couple of times, as if he was trying to grasp the meaning of what he had said just now. He had been here for over two months in all, and loved every moment of it. 'Care to join me for a drink? I still have the last two bottles of Burgundy left, I think.'

'I wouldn't mind doing that.' Roy had finally made peace with Pierre. Maybe at first he had been a little too hard on him. Maybe he wasn't a paedophile at all, but just fond of children. 'Yes…the last drink together. Why not! But, how about the rest?'

'The rest,' Pierre pondered for a while. 'Not much of the rest left, barring you and Billy. Billy should be coming any moment now.'

A minute later Billy came out of the room and joined them. They sat down on the semi-dark balcony and drank.

'No proper wine glasses…sorry about that.'

'Doesn't matter. Cheers!' All three raised their glasses. 'Here's to Pierre's magnum opus!'

Roy took a sip. Even without proper glasses the wine tasted just as good.

'I hope they wouldn't mind.' Pierre looked in the direction of the monks' quarters. 'It's just for one evening.'

The evening was unusually quiet. No one spoke much. As though the ghosts of Miriam and Tenzing were still weighing heavily on their minds.

'Here…have some cheese.' There was a slab of mozzarella on a plate, and a knife to cut it into cubes.

Billy, normally a big eater, just nibbled at it. It was clear he didn't have an appetite. Nobody did.

'So, Billy, when are you going back home?' Pierre asked. 'When I leave tomorrow you will be the only one left. Only one of the foreign legions. Roy…you don't count. You are a native.'

Billy stared vaguely at the distant mountains and shook his head.

'I don't know.' He put a cheese cube in his mouth and munched thoughtfully. 'It all depends.'

Roy looked at him understandingly. He knew Billy had run

away from home, from his insatiable wife. Pierre, perhaps, didn't know that.

'Any progress on Miriam's murder? That witch of a nun!' Pierre's hatred for the nun was understandable. 'Unless, of course, it's all classified information.'

That Roy was a senior detective officer from Kolkata was no more a secret now. Most people at the monastery also knew that for the last couple of days he had been assisting inspector Thapa in trying to solve the mystery surrounding the twin murders at Dengziang. Indeed, Roy had expected that this question would crop up sometime that evening.

'What we've been able to piece together so far is that the nun may not be a nun at all, but a man; a man who has been trained to be a ruthless assassin.'

'But why did he have to come here, of all places, and go on a killing spree?'

'Perhaps, he came here in search of something. Maybe Miriam somehow got involved in this, we don't know for sure.'

'Miriam getting involved with a trained assassin? That's hard to believe,' Billy shook his head.

'I agree. But circumstances have been known to force people to do stranger things.'

'Has this man been caught yet?'

'No, but speaking strictly in confidence, Thapa and his team are doing whatever it takes to apprehend him before he vanishes into thin air. Make no mistake, this man is as elusive as a chameleon.'

'All very cloak and dagger!' Billy said ironically.

'But why are you here, then?' Pierre turned abruptly to Roy. 'You should've been there with them now, in the thick of things.'

'Perhaps, but maybe I'm getting on in years. Maybe I'm no more cut out for hot pursuits through dense jungles at night. Not on foot, anyway.'

'And you Pierre...you're so fond of children. Why didn't you ever get married, then? One would've imagined that you would be the first person to get married and beget children by the dozen.' Pierre's being a bachelor was a well-known fact.

'Ah well. I never probably found the woman willing to bear those brats for me.'

'Or maybe you fell in love and got ditched. As they say, once bitten, twice shy.'

Hearing footsteps behind them they turned around. It was the waiter from the dining room.

'Sir, dinner's been ready for a while. Maybe you would care to come down and join the rest.'

'Thanks. In a minute.'

The waiter threw an ironic glance at the two bottles on the table and left.

'To hell with the dinner. Let's get merrily drunk tonight.'

As Pierre was pouring fresh drinks into the glasses Billy's telephone rang, startling everyone. No one had seen him receiving or making phone calls before. Billy frowned as he looked at the number flashing on the screen.

'Excuse me,' he picked up the cell phone and walked away to the farthest end of the passage. It was clear he didn't want anyone to overhear the conversation. Roy looked curiously at Billy's receding figure.

As the evening wore on everyone got drunk silly. Billy, who had a way of managing things around there ordered for heaps of pork sausages and ham to go with the drinks. After polishing off both the bottles, they decided to go out for a walk. It was a moonlit night. After many days Roy felt happy, even euphoric. He knew it was all due to the Burgundy wine. He also knew he would wake up the next day with a bloated stomach and a blinding headache. Wines inevitably caused him acidity and heartburn.

Suddenly, out of nowhere, a motorcycle zoomed past them. It was a heavy bike, not the stuff that they manufactured these days, the engine making a solid 'boom boom' sound. Even in the darkness Roy could decipher two hefty figures mounted on the bike, their faces hidden by large goggles.

'Good bike that,' Billy turned around in appreciation. 'Could be a Harley or, maybe a Sunbeam.'

'You like bikes a lot, don't you?' Pierre enquired.

'Like them? I simply love' em. Had a 12 horsepower monstrous Harley at one time. I tell you, the wind blowing through your hair, the black road surging past under your wheels…there's no feeling on earth that can quite match it.'

But, for some reason that he couldn't quite explain, Roy was filled with an unknown apprehension. The last thing that crossed his mind before he fell blissfully asleep was what on earth that bike was doing there, outside the monastery, in the middle of the night.

That morning was a different day. The leaves looked translucent and glowing, like tiny bulbs, backlit by the sun. The fog floated about in soft blue coils. Dewdrops, collecting at the end of leaves, stayed suspended mid-air, defying laws of gravity.

Antonio felt refreshed and almost cheerful as he walked down the trail. In broad daylight everything looked so crystal clear. The trail was well marked and well trodden. He had no idea why he had felt so vulnerable and insecure last night. Maybe because he had never been faced with this kind of a situation before. Not in such an alien terrain, at least.

Dafeybhir, he reckoned, was just about 10–12 kilometres from there. So, two more hours of brisk walk like this and he should be at the border of Sikkim and Nepal. Last night his meeting with the Lepcha villager had been really fortuitous. When he had seemingly lost his way in the forest, this man had appeared, lantern in hand, out of nowhere.

That man lived a strange life, he thought. His cottage was in the middle of the forest, with no other human habitation within miles. As for his son, he didn't seem to go to any school. Did he have a wife? If so, where? How did this man eke out his living? As a woodcutter? Antonio had meant to ask him all these questions. But language had acted as an impregnable barrier, stone-walling all his questions.

In exchange of a few hundred rupees the villager had provided him shelter in the tiny outhouse of his for the night. He had even provided a thick, coarse blanket that had protected him from the bitter cold that seemed to emanate from the earth underneath like some deathly sulphuric vapour. But, in spite of all this he hadn't slept well. The wind had howled through the night, rattling the rickety window and door of his room. There were other unexplained sounds that surrounded the hut. He thought he heard footsteps on dry leaves, as if they were circling his room. At one time he seemed to hear a gentle knock on the door. He had stealthily got up from the charpoy and tiptoed to the door, listening. But there was no movement outside. He had suddenly jerked open the door, the Swiss knife poised in hand. But there was no one to be seen, no sound, not even an owl hooting.

The rest of the night he had dozed, on and off, half lying on the charpoy, having weird dreams that he couldn't remember in the morning. He had left the cottage long before dawn, slipping another 500-rupee note inside the folds of the blanket and latching the outer door shut. But the Lepcha had woken up even before, and was in the opening in front of the cottage, felling logs. When he saw Antonio, he gave him a broad grin.

'Chai?'

At least Antonio knew this word. He shook his head. God knows how much time he would take preparing it? He didn't want to get unnecessarily delayed in the morning.

But, why was the woodcutter being so helpful? Antonio had asked himself. Suspicious by nature, he had questioned the motive behind last night's meeting with this guy. How could he have appeared out of nowhere, just like that? Did the woodcutter have an inkling of who he was? In which case, he could have informed the police. All these questions had raged through his mind. He looked at the fellow carefully. Was he a police informer? No, he decided at length. The chap's smile was so guileless, he couldn't really be.

And he reasoned, had this fellow been a police informer, by now the cottage would've been surrounded by a posse of policemen. And he would have been surely arrested. Arrest him? He smiled. Nobody was ever going to arrest him alive.

'You have a cell phone?' He lifted the cupped hand to his ear, miming a phone call.

Surely the woodcutter, even if he lived in the middle of a forest, knew of cell phones. If he had any in his possession he could be passing on information to the police. In that case, Antonio would have no choice but to kill him, irrespective of the fact that he had a small kid without a mother.

In response to his question the woodcutter pulled his pant pockets inside out and gave a toothy grin.

'*Itna paisa kahan?*'

It was true; this guy lived in abject poverty.

'Well then goodbye and thank you for everything.' He took out another 500-rupee note from his wallet and gave it to him. 'This one's for your kid.'

Not too sure if the man had understood him, he had indicated with his hand the size of the kid.

'I better get moving now,' he told himself, and left.

Since then, Antonio had been walking for a long time, except for a brief break, a few gulps of water and a slab of cheese. The sun had gone considerably higher up, making the day warmer. So he unzipped the front of his padded windcheater and breathed more easily. On the way, nothing much had happened. A few stray local people had passed him by, saying 'salam', and raising their hand.

Other than that, nothing.

The morning haze had lifted. From where he was standing, he thought he could spot the village of Dafeybhir. So he was almost there. From this height he could make out a gorge ahead. But how did one cross it? His eyes followed the length of the gorge to spot a narrow bridge on the left. So that's where he should be heading. In racing parlance, he had hit the last straights. Suddenly he felt elated and started whistling.

Roy had been meaning to pay a visit to the private monastery of Suraj Rumba for some time now. The enlightening experience of that particular morning had stayed with him all those days, prompting him to visit the place once again. But the quick sequence of events, happening one after the other over the last week, had conspired against his doing so.

That morning, however, he was comparatively free and decided to visit the place. But, before he could do that he had some unfinished business at Pelling, some residences to visit, several people to talk to and discreet enquiries to make. Accordingly, he arranged for a cab and went to the town. His enquiries in the township had gone off unexpectedly well. So he was coming back in a rather cheerful frame of mind. He paid off the cab as he neared Rumba's residence and went down the steps through the wood to his favourite place of solitude. Mr Rumba wasn't present this time. But, his servant was gracious enough to open the monastery for him.

'You want some tea?' the attendant had asked him, knowing how his master would have liked him to have a cup.

Roy politely declined the offer.

He had gone up to the first floor, climbing the steep staircase, and reached the prayer hall. He had sat down cross-legged as before. The hall was still just as cool and quiet. But there was no magical light coming through the small grill near the roof that day. And somehow, it felt rather damp and dusty.

After a while he came out of the monastery, told the attendant he was leaving, and found his way back to the main road. Dengziang was only a walking distance from there. The solitude of the monastery lasted through the road. There was not a soul around. No pedestrians, no cars.

He walked down the middle of the road, found a pebble to kick around, just as he used to do as a small boy. The trick was to keep the pebble as long in play as possible. As he was engrossed in playing pebble soccer, he heard a motorcycle approaching from behind. He left the pebble on the road and stood aside to let the bike pass. To his utter surprise he found it heading straight towards him. Mounted on the bike were two hefty guys, their faces almost masked by large pairs of goggles. He remembered seeing those two figures, mounted on the same bike, the night before as he, along with Pierre and Billy, were having an after-dinner stroll. Only difference, it wasn't going to be a stroll for him today.

The bike gathered speed and came straight at him. Big guys, on a big bike. The pillion rider flashed a dagger, his arm coming out in a wide, sweeping arc aimed at his midriff.

In a way, Roy had a strange premonition that something of this nature was going to happen to him. Subconsciously he had been dreading it from the very day that huge boulder of rock had come hurtling down on him and Miriam. He knew there would be another attempt on his life. Miriam was already dead. So was Tenzing. He was, as it were, the last in the list of 'wanted deads'.

Roy had nowhere to go. He had stood aside on the open side of the road to let the bike pass. Now, they had cornered him, cutting his way off. He started running away, in a zig zag movement. But the roar of the engine was upon him in no time. From the corner of his eye he could just make out the shining dagger coming at him in a flash. At the very last moment, he jumped away from the road. It was virtually a free fall, the land sloping away at a more than 45 degree angle.

He desperately tried to grasp at anything, tufts of grass, saplings, jutting out rock formations, anything at all, as he slid fast down the precipice. Unfortunately, there was nothing much to hold on to. Suddenly, he felt his body thud against something solid. He felt a searing pain on his ribs. Nonetheless, he blindly reached out with his hands and they stuck. Miraculously, he wasn't falling any more. He looked around to find himself hanging perilously from the branch of a tree. As he looked down he had the briefest glimpse of a road snaking away, some 50 feet below. Roy shivered, this time in genuine fright. He suffered from vertigo.

Hanging from the branch like this, Roy wouldn't have normally survived too long. But, the last three weeks in the hills, with its long walks on mountainous roads, had toughened his body, so that he actually managed to swing away to the comparative safety of the main tree.

Just then he heard a voice from above.

'Sir, are you all right?'

Roy let out a frightened grunt in response.

'I'm throwing down a length of rope to you. Do you think you could catch and hold onto it?'

It was Pradyot's comforting voice, coming from above. Within ten minutes Roy had been hauled up to safety.

'What took you so long in coming?' Roy said, fuming with anger as he dusted the lapel of his jacket. 'I thought you were supposed to be my shadow, covering my back.'

'Entirely my fault, sir,' Pradyot admitted ruefully. 'But, everything happened so fast, I just couldn't make it in time.'

Roy glared at Pradyot in response. Never in his life did he have such a close shave with death. Inside, he was still shaking like an aspen leaf.

'Sir... would it be terribly impertinent if I asked you a question?'

'Well... what is it?' Roy looked at his assistant suspiciously.

Pradyot stood at the edge of the precipice, looking down at the tree far below.

'Is that your usual hangout, sir?'

Just before Dafeybhir there was a tiny hamlet. It was so tiny, the route map didn't even mention it by name. The trekking route didn't actually run through it. But it was close enough for him to see the smoke coming out of the cottages. He saw a boy guiding a herd of buffaloes to the nearest grazing ground, and a group of lads playing football in a small, grassless clearing. He had been tempted to stop by for a cup of chai. He rather liked the way the locals made their tea there; putting tea leaves, milk and sugar in the water and boiling them all together. But he kept on walking. The sooner he crossed over to Nepal, the safer it would be for him.

And then, without warning it happened. They dropped down from the trees like monkeys, snub-nosed, slit-eyed Gurkhas. And in no time at all, they were all around him, two to three people, forming a phalanx and closing in steadily. They were armed with what these villagers called kukris, daggers with deadly curved blades.

Antonio thought he was having a bad dream. Surely this couldn't be for real. Then a short, stocky man stepped out from the group and shouted at him.

'Antonio Vitolo, your game is up.'

Who was this pot-bellied clown with blood shot eyes? How did he know his name? This was weird. Because, when he left Pelling he was absolutely certain there wasn't anyone tracing his footsteps. Then how could this guy have come here, with so much back-up support? And this chap obviously knew he would be taking this route. How was that possible? He had confided in no one.

'I think you've got it all wrong. Who this Antonio guy is, I have no idea.'

The unfortunate thing was he had no firearms with him. He had entered India officially, having his passport duly stamped at the airport. He could've of course purchased a gun illicitly from the local market, but had refrained from doing so. He didn't wish to draw unnecessary attention to himself.

'We know who you are. You've been single-handedly

responsible for the gruesome murder of two Indian citizens, Miriam de Gonzales and Tenzing Thorpa. And what makes these murders even more heinous is that you've committed them inside the holiest of places, a Buddhist monastery. After committing these murders you've run away from Pelling and are about to cross over to Nepal. But I will never let that happen. Nobody escapes after committing a murder in my beat.'

'Yes,' Antonio raised his arms in a gesture of appeasement. 'I'm coming from Pelling all right. But beyond that nothing else fits. These names that you mention…far from murdering them, I don't even know who they are.'

The pot-bellied man simply laughed and shook his head.

'It's best that you surrender to us. And the law of the land will then decide on your fate. Who knows, they might even spare your life. Or else,' at this point this chap fished out a gun from somewhere, 'it would give me the greatest pleasure to shoot you down. The process will be long and I'll go out of my way to make it very very painful, I promise you that.'

Antonio looked about him. Hostile faces were all around and inching closer and closer. He simply shrugged, smiled and took the only course left open to him. He did an about turn and ran full tilt towards the gorge. Before anyone could even bat an eyelid, he had dived into the precipice. Inspector Thapa ran as fast as he could and looked down. It was a sheer fall of at least 500 feet. He could see a mountain river flowing far below, at torrential speed. There was white foam churning as the river lashed against the protruding rocks. There was no earthly chance that any human being could possibly survive such a steep fall.

Roy was down on the road again, all by himself. He could've easily had Pradyot tag along with him. But that would have defeated the very purpose of the move. They had attacked him once. And, chances were, they were going to attack him again. They were only waiting for an opportunity to find him alone.

Roy and Pradyot had rehearsed the plan over and over again. So that when they came for him this time Pradyot would be ready.

'Are you sure you've never seen them before?' Pradyot had asked Roy after he had been rescued that morning.

'I don't know. I might've seen them without noticing them. Except for last night.'

Roy had then told his assistant how two men on a bike had crossed them as he was taking a stroll last night with Billy and Pierre.

'And you're sure that these two are the same men?'

'I think so. And I have a feeling that this isn't the first time they've mounted an attack on me.'

'What do you mean?'

'This happened some time ago, before you came here. I was returning from Pelling with Miriam one afternoon when a huge boulder came rolling down, all but crushing us to a pulp. It was a plan to murder us, made to look like an accident. And my gut feel is they are the same chaps who did this.'

'But why should they want to murder you?'

'That's the big question. My presence here isn't being liked by some people, that is for certain.'

At one time they had even thought of waiting for Inspector Thapa to return before taking any precipitate action on their own. That was another thing bugging him. Thapa hadn't called back or contacted him since the day before, when the police had mounted an all-out effort to apprehend Antonio. At the last moment he had decided not to join the manhunt. And he was right. His weary body didn't have it in him to carry out the arduous chase through dense jungles at night anymore.

So, the choice was, either stay away from the streets or come out in the open, drawing them out in the process.

Also, the attack on him had incensed Roy. It wasn't so much a question of taking revenge (he was too old for that), as a refusal to be cowed down by these hooligans, whoever they might be.

So, here he was, out in the open and alone, offering himself as a soft target, as bait. And just to show his mental composure, he started whistling again. And it had to be 'rain drops keep falling on my head'. Quite ridiculous really, but, for the life of him, he couldn't think of any other tune at that very moment.

As he walked down the empty road he could sense something was going to happen now. His animal instincts warned him, making his neck muscles taut without any apparent reason. And, sure enough, before long he could hear the deep 'boom boom' of the motorcycle, echoing and re-echoing on the walls of the hills, though he couldn't sight it actually.

Trouble was he couldn't be sure which side it was coming from. The echo made it impossible for him to determine that. He stood still for a while, trying to make out. Last time they had attacked him from behind. But suddenly he realized he had been fooled. The bike was actually coming from the front and he didn't know it till the moment it had made its appearance from the curve ahead. And then it was too late.

From the hill top, where he had positioned himself, Pradyot had a commanding view of the entire region. He had the telescopic rifle, with its cross-hairs, trained on the road. It wouldn't take him more than a second to aim at any moving target and shoot. He had been there for more than an hour now; even before Roy had stepped out of the monastery.

Luckily, he had brought the long range gun for this trip. Which is why, when coming to Pelling, he had avoided the flight to Bagdogra. The fact that he was carrying a telescopic rifle was best kept a secret.

At around the same time that Roy had heard it, Pradyot too heard the sound of the approaching bike. He had chosen the vantage position on the hill top, based on the thinking that the bike was going to come from behind. And now, at the last moment he realized he was wrong. It was coming from the opposite direction. And his view of the road was obstructed by an intervening tree. Which meant that this very moment, Roy was there all by himself, facing these two professional killers, without any protective cover.

Gun in hand, he ran out of his hiding place, sliding down the slope of the hill, frantically trying to get a proper view of the road. As he was careening dangerously down the loose rubble, he had a momentary view of the bike charging towards Roy. If something were to happen to his boss now, he would never be able to forgive himself. Cursing himself for not choosing a hideout closer to the road, he half-ran, half-slid down, till he tumbled onto the main road. In a flash he was up on his feet, picking up the gun in his hand.

Roy had been right. There were two of them on the bike. One of them, the pillion rider, was brandishing a large kukri in his hand. By the time he had been able to train the gun on them, the bike riders were already upon Roy. The target and Roy were in such close proximity that he dared not take aim and shoot.

At the last moment he watched Roy duck under the pillion

rider's charge. But this guy seemed to have anticipated the move before hand and accordingly lowered the swing of his arm. The force of the hit swung Roy mid-air, turning him turtle. There was a deep gash on his jacket as he lay prone on the road. Having made the sortie, the speeding bike screeched to a halt and wheeled around, raising a cloud of dust. The rider kept the bike still for a moment, revving up the engine all this while, deciding on what to do. With a deafening roar the bike now surged forward, coming straight at Roy. Pradyot had no doubt about the rider's intentions. They wanted to run over his boss' prone body.

Going down on one knee, he took careful aim. The headlight of the bike came in between the cross-hairs and he pressed the trigger. Next moment there was a mini explosion, and he could clearly see the rider lose his balance, as shards of broken glass rained down upon them. The front tyre lost grip and slid badly, careening off the street. Moments later he could hear a loud crash as the bike went down the hill.

He ran towards Roy, his heart in his mouth. He knelt down by his side and gently turned him around. With a huge sigh of relief he realized the latter was breathing, even if somewhat unevenly. Part of his face was covered with cakes of dust.

'Sir…sir can you hear me?' He cushioned his boss' head in his arms and asked softly.

Gradually, Roy groaned back to consciousness. As soon as he had opened his eyes he tried to get up, but was restrained by his assistant.

'What's the matter with you? Let me get up,' he said gruffly.

'You've been hurt, sir.'

It was only then that Roy looked down at himself and noticed the gash. He slipped his right hand inside his jacket and when he brought it out there was blood in his hand.

'Ah well…help me up, then. I only hope there are no broken bones.'

As Pradyot did so, he saw a shadow creep up from behind him on the road. He turned around and could scarcely believe his own eyes. One of the men on the bike was standing directly behind him. Half of his face had been blown off. There was a deep gash on where his right eye should have been. Blood was still spurting out from several wounds in his body. But, somehow, even in this condition he had managed to crawl out of the gorge and at that very moment was poised to bring down the kukri on Pradyot with whatever force he could muster.

Instinctively, Pradyot raised the gun and pumped in two quick shots, one after the other, into the assailant's body from point-blank range. The sheer force of the shots threw the assailant some distance away, to the edge of the road. Pradyot got up and stood over the body, the gun still in hand. There was the faintest twitch on the assailant's left toe, and then the body went still.

In the meantime Roy had somehow managed to get up from the road and was trying to make a sling out of his comforter to rest his left hand on. When Pradyot went back to him he found the latter grumbling away. 'What is it, sir?'

The old man seemed to get easily crotchety these days.

'Well, don't you see what they've done?' Roy was fuming. 'The bloody sods, they've ruined my Harrod tweed jacket!'

Pradyot didn't know whether to laugh or cry. Here was this man who's just had the closest shave with death and all he could think of was his ruined tweed jacket!

Next morning Roy finished breakfast early and got ready to go out. At 9 a.m. there was a knock on his door. It was Inspector Thapa's driver. Late last night he had received a text message from the inspector, saying it would be great if he could come over to the police station. There was important information to share with him.

When he and Pradyot reached the police station Thapa was his usual terse, laconic self.

'How's the injury?' Thapa looked pointedly at the sling on Roy's left arm. 'Hope it's nothing serious.'

'No, no, nothing more than a graze, I assure you,' Roy played it down. 'But how did you manage to know about it? You weren't even in town at the time.'

'So you see…nothing escapes my attention in Pelling.' There was a mischievous gleam in Thapa's eyes. 'Mr Roy, I've got some good news for you. First, Antonio Vitolo. Your thinking was spot on. He was actually heading for Nepal, via Dafeybhir. And we managed to corner him before he could cross over.'

'You've caught him!' Roy asked excitedly.

'Well, not quite. He eluded arrest by leaping into a 500 feet deep gorge.'

'Did you find the body?'

'No, it was washed away by the turbulent river down below.'

Noticing the scepticism on Roy's face he said, 'Don't worry, we're sure to find his corpse somewhere downstream.'

'But how did you manage to get his whereabouts? Much of the trekking route between Pelling and Dafeybhir is covered by dense forests.'

'We may be small town people with limited resources, but, we try to make up for it by being ingenious,' Thapa said with modest pride. 'After you left, I got in touch with the DM and, through his good offices, managed to send a description of our Antonio to all the village "mukhias" between Pelling and Nepal. Not all of them had cell phones with them, but many did. We figured it would be very difficult, if not impossible, for Antonio to escape our dragnet if our mukhias cooperate.'

'As simple as that?'

'The idea might look simple. But the execution wasn't. We had to monitor the entire process of making the calls ourselves. And the poor mukhias, they had to mobilize manpower within hours to keep an eye on this man. And this carried on through the entire night.'

Roy had to admit the idea was brilliant in its simplicity.

'And when did you make your first contact?'

'Oh that! Through a woodcutter who lives deep inside the forest. He was quite smart really. He conducted the search taking his young lad with him. Now who would ever suspect a poor man with a small boy to be on the lookout for a dangerous international criminal?' Thapa permitted himself a smile here. 'But, we had strict instructions that no one should try to take any action on his own.'

'Well that's great! I'm happy for the sake of Miriam and Tenzing, if nothing else.'

'But there's more news. It's to do with your assailants.'

'What about them?'

'Well, from whatever information we've been able to dig out so far, it would seem they aren't from here at all, but from as far away as Ladakh.'

'Ladakh?' Roy couldn't contain his surprise.

'Yes, that's what we've gathered from some papers found on one of them. Any idea as to why someone should come all the way from Ladakh to kill you?'

'No,' Roy said scratching his head. 'No idea at all.'

Thapa's eyes were narrowed to a slit as he kept staring at Roy.

'And Antonio…why did he come to Pelling? Just to murder Miriam and Tenzing?'

Roy simply shook his head.

'I see,' Thapa said abruptly. 'You won't tell me.'

'No no, it's not like that at all. I would tell you, if I knew for certain.'

'And how much longer are you going to be here, Mr Roy?'

'That I certainly can, tell you' Roy said, smiling. 'My private business is virtually over. So, I should be leaving in a day or two.'

This time it was Pradyot who looked surprised at his boss.

On the way back Pradyot couldn't contain his curiosity anymore.

'Sir, we haven't made any headway on the manuscript as yet and you told him we're leaving in a day or two? I just don't understand this!'

'Yes, so I said,' Roy answered with an enigmatic smile. The rest of the trip he discussed everything under the sun other than the missing manuscript. Having reached the monastery he took the staircase. 'Let's go to my room. I'm dying for a cup of coffee.'

Pradyot didn't say a word. At times Roy liked to play a deliberate waiting game.

Coffee mugs in hand, they stood at the balcony. The courtyard below wore a deserted look. After the Tenzing incident the kids had all been sent home and weren't likely to return too soon. A few lamas went about their daily chores quietly. They spotted Lama Chorten cross the courtyard and walk towards his room.

'I think we'll go and have a word with him now,' Roy said.

'Lama Chorten!' Roy called up from behind as the former was entering his room.

Chorten turned around, surprised.

'Can we have a quiet word with you?'

'Certainly.' Chorten stood aside to let them in. 'Sorry, my room is so small.'

Roy sat on the only chair in the room. Pradyot occupied the low mattress. Chorten stood leaning against the wall. Roy let the awkward silence persist.

'Yes, Mr Roy...you wanted to say something?'

Roy kept silent for a while. 'I think an honest confession is called for.'

'Honest confession...' Chorten looked surprised. 'I don't understand.'

'You tell me.' Roy looked back sharply at him. 'I think you understand very well what I am talking about.'

Chorten shook his head. 'No, I really don't.'

If Roy had meant to ruffle him up, it didn't work. Chorten remained his usual serene self.

'I think you need to return the Issah manuscript. Lama Phunsok has been punished enough for whatever hurt he might have caused you in the past.'

'Issah manuscript...what are you talking about?'

'Don't you now?' Roy's voice hardened noticeably. 'No use pretending with me. I know exactly what happened in the past. And I know that the manuscript is right now in your possession.'

Chorten looked defiantly back at Roy. 'You have no proof, nothing.'

'Listen, Chorten, I've been to your home, talked to your parents. They've told me everything. From how you'd been brutalized when you were very young. And how you are harshly punishing that person back now.'

Chorten still remained silent. But now you could make out that a whole lot of thoughts were churning in his mind.

'They told me about the time when you carried the manuscript home for copying. They asked you pointedly as to why you were doing it. And you didn't answer. But they're honest, morally upright people. They guessed what you are doing and they don't approve of it at all.'

The young lama sighed deeply, his eyes glistening.

'I don't want to call the police in,' Roy said in the gentlest voice. 'It will help no one, instead cause deep anguish all around.'

Roy got up from his seat and came close to Chorten. 'I think it's time to put it behind you. And take your life forward. It's no use my trying to console you. The scar will remain with you all your life. But you are a good man. With time you should be able to overcome it.'

Chorten turned around, hiding his face against the wall and wept bitterly.

'I'll see to it that nobody else knows anything about it. I promise.' He put his hand gently on the lama's shoulder and said, 'I'm sure you'll be able to put it back where it was. If you can do it tonight, nothing like it. I'll make sure nobody else gets to know about it. Ever.'

That afternoon things happened in quick succession. When Roy went back to his room, he found a sealed envelope under the door. He opened it to find a brief note from Billy with some money in it. It had apparently been written in great hurry. It said he had had to leave the monastery because of a personal emergency. The money left behind should suffice in meeting his dues at the guesthouse. The nature of the emergency was, however, left unexplained.

Within an hour of receiving the note a tall lady with an Anita Ekberg figure showed up at the monastery without warning. She claimed Billy was her absconding husband and that she had been frantically looking for him for the past three months. And that only recently she had received definitive information that he was staying in Pelling.

Billy of course was nowhere to be found. Nobody knew where he had gone, or when he would return, if at all. She came upstairs and went over to the corner room where Billy had lived all this time. The room was empty. Billy had cleared out with everything. She then stormed into Roy's room without knocking, putting him into considerable discomfiture.

'I believe you are Billy's friend.'

Roy merely nodded in answer. Even from a distance one could feel the aura of her sexuality.

'Any idea as to where he might've gone?'

Roy shook his head. She looked around her, taking in Roy's belongings.

'Mind if I sit down here and chat for a while? I'm tired.'

'Unfortunately I have to go out and meet some people urgently.'

'I see.' She looked hard at him and stormed out of the room without another word.

The elusive couple that Roy had so detested in the past had returned to the monastery. The depressed, mousy-looking wife was in raptures. Apparently, they had been in correspondence with an NGO organization in Sikkim for a long time regarding the adoption of a baby. At long last their dream had been fulfilled. They had successfully negotiated with a Lepcha family there for the adoption of one of their babies.

In the evening Roy went up to meet with Lama Phunsok.

Seeing him, the old man hurriedly closed the door behind him and asked, 'Mr Roy, have you got any good news for me?'

Roy smiled and nodded.

Lama Phunsok took a couple of steps forward and looked at his face searchingly.

'You really mean it?'

'Yes.'

The elderly lama came forward and clasped his hands warmly, almost hugging him.

'Where...where is it?'

'Not with me just now. But, tomorrow, should you look for it in the underground vault, it will be there. Exactly where it was.'

'How can you be so certain? How did you find it? Who took it away? Please tell me everything.'

Roy's face had turned grave. 'That's something that I can't do.'

The venerable lama was about to say something, but Roy shook his head firmly.

'There is a condition attached. You will not ask me anything more on the subject.'

Lama Phunsok looked somewhat crestfallen, but thanked him again and again.

'Mr Roy. You've saved my reputation, no...more than that. You've saved my very life.'

Roy shook off the compliment, embarrassed. 'If you don't mind, I shall be leaving tomorrow.'

'But of course. You've had to extend your stay for so many days on my account. How can I ever repay your debt?'

'You don't have to.' Roy gently disengaged his hand from Lama Phunsok's. 'A couple of questions before I go. Hope you don't mind answering them?'

'No no, please ask.'

'Currently, what is your relationship like with Hemis Monastery?'

A troubled look appeared on the senior lama's face. 'Why do you ask this?'

'I have reasons,' came the enigmatic reply.

'Well…there's been a change of guard in Hemis.' Lama Phunsok let out a deep sigh. 'A new lama has taken charge of the monastery. He is…how should I put it, like a corporate executive, ambitious, aggressive.'

'Has there been any communication with you lately?'

'How did you…?' the senior lama left the question incomplete.

'Just guessing.'

'There's been a personal communication from him very recently. Probably an official letter will follow. They want the Issah manuscript back.'

Roy nodded to himself a couple of times and was quiet for a while.

'And your relationship with the church?'

'You mean the Christian religion? Oh…I get it. Are you thinking of what impact this secret manuscript is likely to have on them? Well, officially we deny that any such document exists at all. We do not in any way want to hurt the sentiments of other religions, certainly not that of Christians. We know Jesus Christ died as a Buddhist. That's enough for us.'

'That's all, Lama Phunsok,' Roy got up to leave. 'Oh! Just a matter of detail, what do you want to do with the secret surveillance system covering the monastery?'

'I don't think we require it anymore.'

Roy nodded and left the room.

That evening Roy called Pradyot over for a drink. They didn't have to appear as strangers anymore. The danger was over. As they sat in the semi-darkness of the first floor balcony, drinking scotch with water, Pradyot couldn't help asking, 'Sir, a few things about this case are still a little unclear to me.'

'I thought as much.' Roy let out a short burst of laughter. 'Okay, shoot.'

Pradyot remained silent for a while, composing the questions in his mind.

'Sir, who exactly was Antonio Vitolo? Who sent him here, and why?'

'I can't give you a very clear cut answer to this. And what I say would be largely conjecture. Is that all right with you?'

'I suppose so.'

'See...there are numerous Orders within the Christian religion. You have the Roman Catholics, Protestants and then, there are so many others—the Anglican Church, The Presbyterian Church— you name it. Antonio could have been sent by one of these Orders to steal the Issah manuscript. I've done a little background research on this. He could've been sent by one of the more esoteric sects within the Christian religion—the Order of the Eastern Star.'

'How did you come to this conclusion, sir?'

'Remember our interview with Lama Tashiding? He had noticed the nun wearing a ring with a special star crest on it. I did a little Google hunting and came up with this name. The Order of the Eastern Star has a star crest as its main emblem.'

'A Christian Order prone to such violence?'

'Why, haven't you read about the Holy Wars in the history book? The crusaders who fought the Holy War were anything but holy. They were mostly soldiers of fortune, mercenaries. What about the burning of so-called heretics and witches during the

Middle Ages? Joan of Arc at the stakes, for instance. So, don't tell me that the church can't be violent.'

'About the assassins from Ladakh…why were they after you?'

'That's more difficult to answer. My gut feel is they had been sent here to retrieve the Issah manuscript at any cost. And I strongly suspect that one or more senior lamas at Dengziang were part of this secret plan. Now when I stayed back at Pelling the inside sources in the monastery must have got fairly alarmed. You see, by now they knew that I was a detective officer from Kolkata. Unless they could get me out of the way, their plans to retrieve the manuscript secretly would've become that much more difficult. Though you can't prove it, the entire thing could have been orchestrated from the Hemis Monastery, in Ladakh. Originally it was their property. And now they want it back.'

Roy remained silent for a while. 'These two chaps could've been plain hired killers. Or they could be 'rogue' monks, lamas who have been thrown out of the religious order because of indiscipline or immoral behaviour. But, they might still have retained tenuous ties with their monastery. And it is entirely possible that two such 'rogue' monks had been especially assigned this task.'

Pradyot thought about the answer for a while and nodded.

'Now to the most important question…how did you figure out that it was Lama Chorten who had committed the theft?'

Roy gave a faint smile before answering. 'I always knew that the theft of the document couldn't have been carried out without inside help. Finally it boiled down to the question of who it was amongst them. It narrowed down to Tenzing, Chorten, Chornum, Tshering and a couple of others. Tenzing was a big suspect. He had a relationship with Miriam and Miriam had presumably been assigned by Antonio to organize the theft through Tenzing. You might not know it, but Lama Tshering and Phunsok are bitter rivals. But Tshering didn't have the manuscript in his possession. If he had, he would have made it public to discredit Phunsok. So, that left just a couple of others, including Chorten. I went over to their households and made enquiries. The copying of the document had to be done away from prying eyes in the privacy of one's home. Lama Chorten's people are highly religious and never approved of their son committing the theft. So, when I questioned them on the subject, they readily confessed the truth.'

'But Chorten didn't do it for money or power. Then what made him do it?'

'When he was very young, just a trainee lama, he might have been abused by Phunsok. I can't tell you the exact nature of that abuse. But it made life absolute hell for him. So much so, that at one time he even contemplated leaving the Order.'

'So, it finally boils down to exacting revenge?'

Roy simply smiled in answer. 'Have another drink before we go down for dinner. Tomorrow we leave early to catch the morning flight from Bagdogra.'

Acknowledgements

Many years ago I read a book that suggested Christ had visited India. At that time the idea had struck me as quite fanciful. But, later on, I came across a BBC documentary that claimed Christ had not only come to India but that he was, in fact , a Buddhist monk. Both these sources indicated the presence of a rare manuscript that chronicles Christ's life in India. This manuscript was supposedly hidden somewhere in a Buddhist Monastery in Ladakh—all very hush hush.

That set me thinking—what if such a document actually exists? Could one write a crime thriller around this secret document? But, my innate lazy self promptly put it on the back burner, baulking at the very thought of undertaking such a formidable project.

However, the final prodding came from an unexpected quarter, a young director friend of mine, named Shubhrajit, who coaxed a four-page synopsis out of me with the promise of making a film out of it. The film never came through. But, the present book did. So, in a way I am indebted to him for writing this book.

Once the first draft was complete two persons contributed enormously in bringing the book to its present shape. The first is my son Avik, a very fine writer in his own right, and one whom I consider to be more of a friend than son. And the other, my drinking pal of many an evening, Shibnath Sen, who so diligently and painstakingly went through the manuscript, correcting the errors and smoothening out the rough edges. To both I owe an evening of Laphroaig.

For helping me out with the French conversations in the book I am truly indebted to Prof. Chinmoy Guha, who so willingly wrote it all down for me over a cup of Cafe' au lait. To Kunal Basu, I am in debt for the generous endorsement on the cover jacket at such a short notice.

For the cover design my indebtedness to two photographer friends of mine, Rohini and Vivek, the former, for providing the picture of a snow-covered river from her Ladakh collection, and the latter, for the beautiful still-life picture of a prayer wheel. And to Raghu, my dear art director friend, for putting it all together and coming up with a brilliant cover design.

At Rupa I am in the thrall of Raju Burman, for all the support and encouragement. And to Rudra Narayan and Nishtha for going through the final proofs with the utmost care and for fine tuning the get up of the book.